Holt Literature & Language Arts

Sixth Course

TEACHER'S NOTES & ANSWER KEY

UNIVERSAL ACCESS Developmental Language & Sentence Skills

Support for *Warriner's Handbook*

Support for Guided Practice in
- **Grammar**
- **Usage**
- **Mechanics**
- **Sentences**

HOLT, RINEHART AND WINSTON

ISBN 978-0-55-401116-5
ISBN 0-55-401116-6

1 2 3 4 5 6 179 13 12 11 10 09

Contents

Chapter 1

PARTS OF SPEECH OVERVIEW: IDENTIFICATION AND FUNCTION

Chapter 2

THE PARTS OF A SENTENCE: SUBJECT, PREDICATE, COMPLEMENT

Chapter 3

THE PHRASE: KINDS OF PHRASES AND THEIR FUNCTIONS

Chapter 4

THE CLAUSE: INDEPENDENT AND SUBORDINATE CLAUSES, SENTENCE STRUCTURE

Chapter 5

AGREEMENT: SUBJECT AND VERB, PRONOUN AND ANTECEDENT

Chapter 6

USING PRONOUNS CORRECTLY: CASE FORMS OF PRONOUNS; SPECIAL PRONOUN PROBLEMS

Chapter 7

CLEAR REFERENCE: PRONOUNS AND ANTECEDENTS

Chapter 8

USING VERBS CORRECTLY: PRINCIPAL PARTS, TENSE, VOICE, MOOD

Chapter 9

USING MODIFIERS CORRECTLY: FORMS AND USES OF ADJECTIVES AND ADVERBS; COMPARISON

Contents

To the Teacher

The worksheets in the student edition are designed for students who should be capable of doing on-grade level English work, but who, for whatever reason, have encountered a grammatical skill or concept that they are having difficulty mastering. You can now intervene by selecting practice exercises designed to help the student master that specific grammatical skill or concept. You can then give the selected worksheets to that student as an extra assignment that complements ongoing class work. Of course, it is important that the student with the deficiency also continue to participate in the regular class work so that he or she does not fall further behind. Worksheets can be used as daily or weekly take-home assignments, or they can be completed during times of the day designated for personal study. Occasionally, a student's grammatical misunderstanding might be so specific that the problem could be solved in one worksheet assignment. Often, however, the worksheet assignments will be more extensive. In fact, some students may rely on the worksheets for continual support throughout the school year.

The worksheets can also be used in conjunction with composition instruction. When a student writes an essay that contains one-too-many errors in the possessive case, for example, you can merely staple a possessive case worksheet to the student's paper to be completed along with the essay corrections. This method allows you to individualize grammatical instruction while you continue discussing the principles of composition with the whole class. It also allows you to help your students see the interdependency of the study of composition and the study of grammar.

Beyond the immediate benefits to your lessons in grammar and in composition, the worksheets can help with the long-term goal of boosting scores on state-mandated tests. In this regard, you will likely discover that even strong students have an Achilles' heel. For these students you can select practice worksheets that will target a particular weakness.

Finally, after a student has completed the selected worksheet assignments and you are fairly confident that he or she has mastered the point of grammar (say, direct objects), it is important to acknowledge the accomplishment publicly. For example, you may be teaching a lesson on adjective clauses. During your discussion, you could call on a student who has mastered direct objects, "Edward, does this adjective clause have a direct object?" Edward gets to demonstrate his new expertise in front of his peers and can feel that he is no longer somehow separated from the mainstream of his classmates. This method will also associate the worksheets in the minds of the students with something positive, rather than with a notion of punishment.

Although the concepts in the following worksheets are presented in a very basic and concrete way, students who are struggling may benefit from an additional step in the teaching process. I have found that when my students and I use a consistent pattern of questions and responses in our discussions of grammar, learning becomes easier. I have incorporated many of these patterns in the sections that follow.

In the following tips to the teacher, you will also notice that I have consistently used one line under the subject, two lines under the verb, parentheses around prepositional phrases, and arrows from all modifiers to the words they modify. I have found that this consistent systematic approach has worked especially well for students who

- have attention-deficit disorder,

- find logical reasoning difficult,

- are generally disorganized,

- find grammar too abstract to remember on a long-term or even a short-term basis.

The use of symbols (underlining, parentheses, and arrows) provides a visual cue that students can use to identify what they already know so that they can then more easily focus on what they don't know.

THE SENTENCE

When I started teaching grammar many years ago, I tended to downplay this topic, thinking that just about everybody knew what a sentence was and could easily identify the subject and the verb. I was so eager to get on to the more sophisticated aspects of grammar that I failed to lay the proper foundation and, consequently, caused unnecessary confusion in my students.

Many of your students may know a sentence when they see one but may be unfamiliar with the vocabulary used to discuss sentences. Familiarizing students with the terms *subject*, *predicate*, and *verb* is essential since these are terms that will be used throughout their study of grammar.

The Subject

I tell students that the **subject** of a sentence is who or what the sentence is talking about. I write a sentence on the board and then ask, "Who or what is this sentence about?" When someone answers correctly, I underline the entire subject with one line, emphasizing the consistent use of this marking system. If the student leaves out part of the subject, I remind him or her to include the subject's modifiers. Next, I ask, "Can anyone show me the main word in the subject, the one that, more than any other word, tells what the sentence is about?" When a student comes up with the answer, I write "*ss*" over the simple subject. So far, the sentence might look like this:

The old road along the coast leads you to the beach.

The Predicate

I explain that a **predicate** is everything that is said about the subject. Continuing with the previous sentence, I ask the class, "What is everything that the sentence says about *the old road along the coast*?" When a student answers correctly, I double underline "leads you to the beach." Then, I explain that, in the predicate, the main word is the **verb,** which tells most about what the subject is doing or being. When a student locates the verb *leads*, I write *v*

over it. Next, on the board, I vary the sentence to look like this:

The old road along the coast is the best way to the beach.

I explain that here the road is not doing anything; the verb *is* just indicates existence.

Next, we turn to **helping (auxiliary) verbs.** I explain that helping verbs can be used with both action and linking verbs, and I give many examples of both. I have found it extremely useful to supply students with a list of helping verbs to memorize:

- These helping verbs will always have a main verb after them: *shall, should, will, would, may, might, can, could, must, ought.*

- These forms of the verb *to be* can be used as helping verbs as well as linking or state-of-being verbs: *be, am, is, are, was, were, being, been, become.*

- These forms of the verb *to have* and *to do* can be used as helping verbs as well as action verbs: *have, has, had* and *do, does, did.*

To help students find the subject and the verb in a sentence, I first stress the importance of understanding what the sentence is saying. Students who are having trouble with this assignment should read each sentence three times before they begin. Then, I ask them to find the verb and underline it twice, not leaving out any part of it. Finally, we ask the subject question (who or what did that [or is that]?) and we draw one line under the answer to that question. It is important to include in the examples some imperative sentences, so that students can work with the understood "you."

Remind students to be on the lookout for interrogative sentences. These sentences often begin with a helping verb, followed by the subject, and then the main verb. For example, "Do you like pasta?" Also, encourage the students to say "subject of the verb" instead of "subject of the sentence" or just "subject." This repetition reinforces the students' understanding of the function of the subject.

If your students have studied prepositional phrases, remind them that the object of a preposition can never be the simple subject. Encourage students to "corral" these phrases by putting parentheses around them. Setting them off from the rest of the sentence at this point helps the students focus more clearly on the simple subject and verb.

PARTS OF SPEECH

Learning the eight parts of speech is important for students because, with this vocabulary, a discussion of other grammatical concepts becomes more productive. However, students must understand that a word's part of speech is usually not rigidly fixed. I show students that the same word can be a different part of speech in a different sentence. The word *down* demonstrates this idea particularly well since it can function as five of the eight parts of speech.

Nouns

Tell students that they can easily remember what a noun is because it begins with the letter *n* and so does the word *name*. A noun names something. A noun is anything you can talk about, including things you can't see, such as love, power, and happiness. Tell students that if they're not sure that a word is a noun in a particular sentence, to put *a* or *the* in front of the word, and if *a* or *the* makes sense, the word is probably a noun.

Pronouns

I motivate students to think about pronouns by pointing out that we use pronouns without even thinking about them. When I give them the sentence, "I bought a pizza; the pizza had mushrooms on the pizza," they can immediately see the usefulness of pronouns. We intuitively prefer, "I bought a pizza; it had mushrooms on it." I show students that they already know how to use pronouns, although they may not understand what a pronoun is: it takes the place of a noun.

Adjectives

Ask students to close their eyes and to picture a pile of books. Then, tell students that each of them probably has completely different books pictured in his or her mind, yet all of them are imagining books. Tell the students they are going to modify, or change, the image they have by adding adjectives to their books. Then say: "thick books." Then, "thick, green books." Then, "thick, green, leather books." Then, "these four thick, green, leather books." All these adjectives have made the noun *books* more specific, by answering the questions, *Which? What kind of?* and *How many?* Be sure not to omit the last example using a number because students may overlook the fact that numbers can be adjectives.

I encourage my students to draw an arrow from the adjective to the noun or pronoun it modifies. To reinforce the meaning of this visual, I tell students that an adjective is like a dog on a leash; it stays close to its master, the noun or pronoun it is describing. Remind students that adjectives are usually right in front of the nouns or pronouns they modify but that they can also follow linking verbs as predicate adjectives.

When you ask a student to tell you why a word is an adjective, encourage this pattern of response: "Because it's not just any old book, it's a green book." "Because it's not just any old dog, it's a shaggy dog." "Because it's not just any old shoe, it's a dirty shoe," and so forth. The repetition of this pattern, however absurd it sounds, effectively instills in the student's mind an understanding of how adjectives function.

Adverbs

Adverbs seem to be the hardest part of speech for students to master. I ask students to be patient. Sometimes learning something worthwhile takes a little time.

After defining the term and giving a few examples of typical adverbs ending in *–ly*, I explain further that an adverb could be any word that answers the question, *How? When?* or *Where?* Continually stress these basic adverb questions. When you ask students why a particular word is an adverb, encourage them to begin their response with the words *because it tells* and then to choose from the questions *How? When?* or *Where?* to complete their answer.

I encourage my students to draw an arrow to the verb, adjective, or other adverb that the adverb is modifying.

I rarely go to the movies.

Rarely do I go to the movies.

I go to the movies rarely.

You can use a pair of sentences, such as the following, to model the distinction between adjectives and adverbs:

She is a *fast* runner.

She runs *fast*.

In both sentences, ask students: Does *fast* answer any of the adjective questions: *Which one? What kind? How many?* Or does it answer any of the adverb questions: *How? When? Where?* Encourage students to draw arrows from *fast* to the word it modifies in each sentence.

Prepositions

First, have students memorize a short list of common prepositions, such as *at, in, on, by, for, from, near,* and *with.* Learning this short list enables students to set up a mental paradigm, which helps them identify new prepositions. Then explain that a preposition shows a relationship between its object and another word in the sentence. Have students hold pencils in their hands. Then say, while you are doing the same thing with your pencil, "Place the pencil **on** your desk, now, **beside** the desk, **under** the desk, **against** the desk, **above** the desk; move the pencil **around** the desk." This kind of physical involvement helps students understand what a preposition does.

Conjunctions

The lesson on coordinating conjunctions seems to be an easy one for most students. (We will save the more difficult subordinate conjunctions for the lesson on adverb clauses.) I usually just remind students to be on the lookout for conjunctions when identifying subjects, verbs, and prepositional phrases. A student who does not read a sentence carefully might be inclined to pick out just half of a compound subject, verb, or object of a preposition.

Interjections

Since interjections are not grammatically connected to the rest of the sentence, they are the easiest part of speech for students to recognize. You may want to have your students memorize the short list of interjections given in the textbook.

COMPLEMENTS

I explain that not all sentences will contain a complement. Some sentences don't need one. Some do. "I sneezed" makes sense all by itself, but "I hit" cries out for another word to answer *What?* or *Whom?* Tell students that this word that completes the meaning of the verb is a complement. It looks like the word *complete,* and that's exactly what a complement does: it completes the meaning of the verb. Remind students that they can help themselves recognize complements by underlining the subject once and the verb twice and by crossing out prepositional phrases.

PHRASES

I begin by explaining that a phrase is a group of words used as a single part of speech.

Prepositional Phrases

Review with students the list of common prepositions. Also, remind them that a preposition shows a relationship between its object and some other word in the sentence. Show students how an object of a preposition answers the question *What?* or *Whom?* when we ask the question in this way: First, say the preposition; then, ask *What?* or *Whom?* On the board, for example, write, "The pencil is on the desk." Then ask, "On what?" Give the answer, "The desk. *Desk* is the object of the preposition." Then, note that the answer to the question, the object, is a noun or a pronoun. Put numerous examples on the board, and in a relaxed atmosphere, check for understanding by calling on individuals to ask and answer the object-of-the-preposition question. Point out that a prepositional phrase begins with a preposition and ends with a noun or pronoun. It includes any modifiers that come between these two parts of speech.

I encourage students to place parentheses around all prepositional phrases. Parentheses here, as in math, indicate that the material within them functions as a single unit. The prepositional phrase (in parentheses) will work as an adjective unit or an adverb unit. I have found that "corralling" prepositional phrases into parentheses greatly facilitates teaching subject-verb agreement and helps to keep students focused on the basic structure of a sentence. Many students over the years have told me that this practice has been useful in helping them to read and understand other school subjects.

After students put parentheses around a prepositional phrase, ask them to draw an arrow from the phrase to the word it modifies. Using pairs of sentences such as the following helps students see the relationship between simple adjectives and adjective phrases.

The *corner* house is hers. [Adjective]

The house (*on the corner*) is hers. [Prepositional phrase used as an adjective]

In the same way, students can learn to see the relationship between adverbs and adverb phrases.

She walked *home*. [Adverb]

She walked (*to her house*.) [Prepositional phrase used as an adverb]

Participial Phrase

Tell students that a participial phrase is a group of words that is used as an adjective. The main word in a participial phrase is the present or past participle form of a verb. To help students identify present and past participles, tell them to look for verb forms that end in *ing*, or *ed*, *n*, or *en*. Then, have students check to be sure the verb form is used as an adjective and not as a noun.

Present Participial Phrase

To help students distinguish between participles used as verbs and participles used as adjectives, use a series of three sentences such as the following.

The frog is **jumping** on the lily pads. [verb]

The **jumping** frog landed in the water. [participle] (Point out to students that it's not just any old frog that landed in the water; it's the *jumping* frog.)

The frog, **jumping on the lily pads,** landed in the water. [present participial phrase, made up of the participle plus a modifying prepositional phrase] (Point out to students again the adjective function of the participial phrase [it's not just any old frog; it's the frog *jumping on the lily pads.*])

You may want to point out at this time that verb forms ending in *ing* can also work as nouns. These nouns are called gerunds, and students will learn about them at another time. Just provide a brief example: *Learning about gerunds* is fun! In this sentence the gerund phrase *Learning about gerunds* is a noun phrase, subject of the verb *is. What* is fun? Learning about gerunds.

Past Participial Phrase

Similarly, we can use a series of three sentences to distinguish past participles used as modifiers from past participles used as verbs.

The branches were **broken** by the wind. (verb)

The **broken** branches lay on the ground. (adjective) [Point out that not just any old branches lay on the ground; they were the *broken* branches.]

The branches, **broken by the wind,** lay on the ground. (past participial phrase) [Point out again that it's not any old branches; it's just the ones that were broken by the wind.]

Infinitive Phrases

When teaching infinitives, I remind the students that one of the characteristics of verbs is tense or time. Unlike a finite, conjugated verb, an infinitive has no time constraints binding it: it is infinite.

After explaining that an infinitive can function as an adjective, adverb, or noun, stress that students can determine how an infinitive is used by asking:

- Does this infinitive answer the adjective questions?

- Does it answer the adverb questions?

- Does it function as a noun, in one of the noun positions in the sentence?

Appositive Phrases

To help your students remember the purpose of an appositive, you can put an equals sign above the first comma in the phrase to reinforce that the phrase equals or means the same thing as the noun or pronoun before it:

=

Mr. Jones, **my brother's teacher,** is going to Spain.

I remind students to think of the commas that come before and after nonessential appositive phrases as handles. They can hold on to both handles and lift the phrase right out of the sentence. A nonessential phrase is an interrupter; it doesn't really need to be there.

CLAUSES

An effective mnemonic device for teaching clauses is a picture of an eagle with its claws outstretched. In one claw it clutches a placard with the word "subject" and in the other claw, a placard with the word "verb." The eagle swoops down on a sentence and grabs the subject with one claw and the verb with the other. Now it has a CLAUSE in its CLAWS! Use the fingers of both hands to make claws that "grab" on to a subject **and** a verb every time the class analyzes a clause. My students never seem to forget this image.

Adjective Clauses

Adjective clauses are fairly easy for students to identify because most begin with relative pronouns. Encourage students to memorize these identifiers. You might want to explain that "relative" refers to how this pronoun relates back to a noun or pronoun in another clause and, thus, ties the adjective clause into that clause.

Be sure that students see the relationship between adjectives and adjective clauses. Use a pair of sentences such as the following to demonstrate the connection.

Our **Florida** relatives are visiting us. [adjective]

Our relatives **who live in Florida** are visiting us. [adjective clause]

To reinforce the concept that an adjective clause functions as a modifier, encourage students to draw an arrow from the adjective clause to the noun or pronoun it is modifying.

Adverb Clauses

Adverb clauses begin with words called subordinating conjunctions. Tell your students that if they memorize a list of common subordinating conjunctions, it will be easy for them to identify adverb clauses. Warn students that several subordinating conjunctions can also be used as prepositions or as adverbs. Therefore, if there is no subject and verb after the subordinating conjunction, there is no clause, and what we thought was a subordinating conjunction is actually a preposition or an adverb.

Have you eaten tofu **before?** [adverb]

We had supper **before the game.** [preposition]

Before we ordered, we asked for some water. [adverb clause]

Using the three sentences above, point out to students the relationship of the adverb clause to the adverb and the adverb phrase. Encourage students to draw an arrow from the adverb clause to the verb, adjective, or other adverb it is modifying.

Once they learn about adverb clauses, I encourage my students to use them often in their writing, especially introductory adverb clauses. These clauses pique the curiosity of the reader and, consequently, make the students' writing more interesting: Starting a sentence with *When they found a small key* makes the reader curious about what might happen next.

AGREEMENT OF SUBJECT AND VERB

This topic is often difficult for students because the idea of singular and plural verb forms is somewhat meaningless to them. It is important to explain that verbs aren't actually singular and plural, but they take a form that goes with a singular or plural subject.

I have found that the following method invariably works if you are consistent in having students do all the steps.

1. Cross out prepositional phrases that come between the subject and the verb:

   One (of the pages) *was* missing.

2. When the simple subject is singular, whether it is a noun or a pronoun, substitute *he*, *she*, or *it* (any one of the three will work).

   (She)
   The girl (with the books) *is* my sister.

3. When the subject is plural, substitute *they*.

   (They)
   The reasons (for his success) *are* easy to see.

4. When the following singular indefinite pronouns are subjects, focus on the singular endings *one* or *body:* **one, everyone, everybody, no one, nobody, anyone, someone, somebody.**

5. When the pronouns *each, either,* or *neither* are subjects, think *each* **one,** *either* **one,** *neither* **one.**

   (Each **one**)
   Each (of the students) *has arrived.*

6. Compound subjects connected by *and* take a plural verb form. Substitute the pronoun *they* for subjects joined by *and.*

   (They)
   The coach and his assistant *attend* every game.

7. For subjects connected by *or* or *nor*, look at the subject closest to the verb. If the subject is singular, substitute *he, she,* or *it.* If the subject is plural, substitute *they.* To make the process even easier, just cross out the other subject(s) and the *or* or *nor.*

   (She)
   The twins or my sister *has* my book.

   (They)
   My sister or the twins *have* my book.

8. *Here, there,* and *where* are almost never subjects. If a sentence begins with one of these words, look for the subject after the verb.

   (They)
   There *are* five women on the committee.

9. If the pronoun *you* is the subject, remember that *you* always takes a plural verb form, even when it refers to one person.

MECHANICS

The rules of mechanics, grammar, and usage are interdependent. Therefore, it is sometimes difficult to come up with mechanics tips or tricks that don't require prior knowledge of grammar and usage. Telling students to use a comma between independent clauses joined by a conjunction always assumes that they can recognize independent clauses and conjunctions. One of the best times to bring up many of the following ideas is during discussion of the associated grammar or usage concept.

Capitalization

Most students have no difficulty recognizing *Jennifer* as a proper noun and *student* as a common noun and are not likely to capitalize such words incorrectly. Some students, though, may have more difficulty applying that principle to inanimate objects. Creating a series of sentences such as the following can help reinforce the concept.

If I had a boat, I would name it

__________________.

A series of sentences like the one above could also be used as additional practice in using italics and quotation marks with titles. Students may be more engaged in learning to capitalize and punctuate names that they have come up with on their own.

Commas

An earlier tip suggested that students think of the commas that come before and after nonessential appositive phrases as handles that can lift the phrase right out of the sentence. This image of commas as handles works equally well with any other nonessential elements. Write a sentence such as the following on the board, with the nonessential clause written well above the rest of the sentence.

> **, which had been hopping from branch to branch,**
> The bird
> began to build its nest.

Alternatively, write the sentence above on strips of paper, one strip for *The bird*, one strip for **, which had been hopping from branch to branch,** and one strip for *began to build its nest,* and have a student or two students pull the nonessential clause out by the handles (the commas).

Spelling

Because rules for spelling are so numerous (and exceptions can seem even more numerous), students may get discouraged by seeing every one of their spelling errors marked in red. For students who misspell many words, you might suggest that they use a spellchecking program or keep a dictionary handy. Concentrate classroom instruction on words that a spellchecking program might overlook, such as *there, their,* and *they're.* If students can master such commonly confused words, they may feel better about having to reach for a dictionary to find the plural spelling of *thesaurus,* for example.

CONCLUSION

These worksheets can benefit struggling students by helping teachers intervene before problems become crises. Because they are relatively easy to administer and evaluate, they can benefit overworked teachers. However, this strategy is only one of many that are available to us, such as using sentences from students' favorite books, magazines, or songs to model grammatical structures, playing quiz-show grammar games, singing, chanting, or rapping out grammar rules or lists, and allowing students who have mastered a point of grammar to tutor those who are having difficulty.

In teaching grammar, we should also take some time to consider the image of ourselves that we present to our students. For example, we might encourage our students to see us as coaches who are teaching them to field the grammar issues they encounter in their writing, but we must eschew any kind of image that suggests a dry-as-dust pedant or the grammar police. We can avoid the negative images if we remember what we are, and are not, trying to do. We are not trying to teach our students to be petty about errors, nor are we trying to get them to look down on those who speak nonstandard English. Rather, we seek to empower students by helping them master basic language skills.

Adapted from Sentence Surgery: A Systematic and Graphic Method of Grammar Instruction *by* **Michèle Beck-von-Peccoz.** *Copyright © 2000 by Michèle Beck-von-Peccoz. Reprinted by permission of the author.*

On the following pages are quick reference charts that you may wish to copy and distribute to your students.

California English–Language Arts Content Standards

Written and Oral English-Language Conventions

The California State Board of Education has adopted a set of standards for achievement in Written and Oral English-Language Conventions. Students will be expected to master these standards for their grade level during the school year. In addition, students will be expected to have mastered the standards from previous grade levels. Standard 1.0 is the same for all three grade levels.

1.0 Students write and speak with a command of standard English conventions appropriate to this grade level.

Grades 11–12:

Grammar and Mechanics of Writing

1.1 Demonstrate control of grammar, diction, and paragraph and sentence structure and an understanding of English usage.

1.2 Produce legible work that shows accurate spelling and correct punctuation and capitalization.

Manuscript Form

1.3 Reflect appropriate manuscript requirements in writing.

Grades 9–10:

Grammar and Mechanics of Writing

1.1 Identify and correctly use clauses (e.g., main and subordinate), phrases (e.g., gerund, infinitive, and participial), and mechanics of punctuation (e.g., semicolons, colons, ellipses, hyphens).

1.2 Understand sentence construction (e.g., parallel structure, subordination, proper placement of modifiers) and proper English usage (e.g., consistency of verb tenses).

1.3 Demonstrate an understanding of proper English usage and control of grammar, paragraph and sentence structure, diction, and syntax.

Manuscript Form

1.4 Produce legible work that shows accurate spelling and correct use of the conventions of punctuation and capitalization.

1.5 Reflect appropriate manuscript requirements, including title page presentation, pagination, spacing and margins, and integration of source and support material (e.g., in-text citation, use of direct quotations, paraphrasing) with appropriate citations.

Content Standards Correlations

This chart shows which content standards are covered by each worksheet.

▶ WORKSHEET:	Gr. 12	Gr. 11	Gr. 10	▶ WORKSHEET:	Gr. 12	Gr. 11	Gr. 10
p.1	1.1	1.1	1.3	p.57	1.1	1.1	1.2
							1.3
p.3	1.1	1.1	1.3	p.59	1.1	1.1	1.2
p.5	1.1	1.1	1.3				1.3
p.7	1.1	1.1	1.3	p.61	1.1	1.1	1.2
p.9	1.1	1.1	1.3				1.3
p.11	1.1	1.1	1.3	p.63	1.1	1.1	1.2
p.13	1.1	1.1	1.3				1.3
p.15	1.1	1.1	1.3	p.65	1.1	1.1	1.2
p.17	1.1	1.1	1.3				1.2
p.19	1.1	1.1	1.3	p.67	1.1	1.1	1.2
p.21	1.1	1.1	1.3				1.3
p.23	1.1	1.1	1.1	p.69	1.1	1.1	1.2
			1.2				1.3
			1.3	p.71	1.1	1.1	1.2
p.25	1.1	1.1	1.1				1.3
			1.2	p.73	1.1	1.1	1.2
			1.3				1.3
p.27	1.1	1.1	1.1	p.75	1.1	1.1	1.2
			1.2				1.3
			1.3	p.77	1.1	1.1	1.2
p.29	1.1	1.1	1.1				1.3
			1.2	p.79	1.1	1.1	1.2
			1.3				1.3
p.31	1.1	1.1	1.1	p.81	1.1	1.1	1.2
			1.2				1.3
			1.3	p.83	1.1	1.1	1.2
p.33	1.1	1.1	1.1				1.3
			1.2	p.85	1.1	1.1	1.2
			1.3				1.3
p.35	1.1	1.1	1.1	p.87	1.1	1.1	1.2
p.37	1.1	1.1	1.1				1.3
p.39	1.1	1.1	1.1	p.89	1.1	1.1	1.2
p.41	1.1	1.1	1.1				1.3
p.43	1.1	1.1	1.1	p.91	1.1	1.1	1.2
p.45	1.1	1.1	1.1				1.3
			1.2	p.93	1.1	1.1	1.2
			1.3				1.3
p.47	1.1	1.1	1.1	p.95	1.1	1.1	1.2
			1.2				1.3
			1.3	p.97	1.1	1.1	1.2
p.49	1.1	1.1	1.1				1.3
			1.2	p.99	1.1	1.1	1.2
			1.3				1.3
p.51	1.1	1.1	1.1	p.101	1.1	1.1	1.2
			1.2				1.3
			1.3	p.103	1.1	1.1	1.2
p.53	1.1	1.1	1.1				1.3
			1.2	p.105	1.1	1.1	1.2
			1.3				1.3
p.55	1.1	1.1	1.2				
			1.3				

Content Standards Correlations (continued)

This chart shows which content standards are covered by each worksheet.

WORKSHEET:	Gr. 12	Gr. 11	Gr. 10
p.107	1.1	1.1	1.2 1.3
p.109	1.1	1.1	1.2 1.3
p.111	1.1	1.1	1.2 1.3
p.113	1.2	1.2	1.4
p.115	1.2	1.2	1.4
p.117	1.2	1.2	1.4
p.119	1.2	1.2	1.4
p.121	1.2	1.2	1.4
p.123	1.2	1.2	1.4
p.125	1.2	1.2	1.4
p.127	1.2	1.2	1.3 1.4
p.129	1.2	1.2	1.1 1.4
p.131	1.2	1.2	1.1 1.4
p.133	1.2	1.2	1.1 1.4
p.135	1.2	1.2	1.1 1.4
p.137	1.2	1.2	1.1 1.4
p.139	1.2	1.2	1.1 1.4
p.141	1.2	1.2	1.1 1.4
p.143	1.2	1.2	1.1 1.4
p.145	1.2	1.2	1.1 1.4
p.147	1.2	1.2	1.1 1.4
p.149	1.2	1.2	
p.151	1.2	1.2	1.1 1.4
p.153	1.2	1.2	1.1 1.4
p.155	1.2	1.2	1.1 1.4
p.157	1.2	1.2	1.1 1.4
p.159	1.2	1.2	1.1 1.4
p.161	1.2	1.2	1.1 1.4
p.163	1.2	1.2	1.1 1.4

WORKSHEET:	Gr. 12	Gr. 11	Gr. 10
p.165	1.2	1.2	1.1 1.4
p.167	1.2	1.2	1.1 1.4
p.169	1.2	1.2	1.1 1.4
p.171	1.2	1.2	1.1 1.4
p.173	1.2	1.2	1.1 1.4
p.175	1.2	1.2	1.1 1.4
p.177	1.2	1.2	1.1 1.4
p.179	1.2	1.2	1.1 1.4
p.181	1.2	1.2	1.1 1.4
p.183	1.2	1.2	1.1 1.2 1.3 1.4
p.185	1.1 1.2	1.1 1.2	1.1 1.2 1.3
p.187	1.1 1.2	1.1 1.2	1.1 1.2 1.3
p.189	1.1 1.2	1.1 1.2	1.1 1.2 1.3
p.191	1.1 1.2	1.1 1.2	1.1 1.2 1.3
p.193	1.1 1.2	1.1 1.2	1.1 1.2 1.3
p.195	1.1 1.2	1.2 1.2	1.1 1.2 1.3
p.197	1.1 1.2	1.1 1.2	1.1 1.2 1.3
p.199	1.1 1.2	1.1 1.2	1.1 1.2 1.3
p.201	1.1 1.2	1.1 1.2	1.1 1.2 1.3
p.203	1.3	1.3	1.5

Chapter 1: Parts of Speech Overview, pp. 1–22

The Noun, pp. 1–2

EXERCISE A

1. Old Faithful, a geyser in Yellowstone National Park, erupts at fairly regular intervals.

2. A forerunner of jazz, ragtime is a musical style that was popular earlier in the century.

3. Nutritionists can help patients plan healthy meals and develop good eating habits.

4. Confucius was a famous teacher and philosopher from China.

5. The audience called for an encore after the pianist walked off the stage.

EXERCISE B

6. A
7. C
8. A
9. C
10. A
11. A
12. C
13. A
14. C
15. C

EXERCISE C

16. COLL
17. COMP
18. COLL
19. COMP
20. COMP

The Pronoun A, pp. 3–4

EXERCISE A

1. Did she [3rd] tell him [3rd] about the emergency procedures?

2. We [1st] often spend our [1st] vacations with them [3rd] in New England.

3. The teacher called out several vocabulary words and asked us [1st] to use them [3rd] in a short story.

4. Does he [3rd] know what time you [2nd] will be arriving?

5. A snake had shed its [3rd] skin, which we [1st] found lying on the ground.

6. For dedicating her [3rd] life to the poor, Mother Teresa received the 1979 Nobel Peace Prize.

7. He wore his [3rd] favorite shirt to their [3rd] party. [He = 3rd]

8. I [1st] have finished the book, so you [2nd] may have it [3rd] now.

9. Robert Fulton not only made the steamboat a success, but he [3rd] also designed a submarine and a steam warship.

10. They [3rd] bought a barn and converted it [3rd] into a workshop.

EXERCISE B

11. INT
12. INT
13. INT
14. REF
15. REF

The Pronoun B, pp. 5–6

EXERCISE A

1. that
2. This
3. those
4. That
5. This
6. this
7. these
8. These
9. that
10. those

EXERCISE B

11. Is that [DEM] a blackberry or a dewberry?

12. Whose [INT] is the abstract painting on the far wall of the gallery?

13. Are those [DEM] Calvin's computer magazines?

DEM
14. <u>That</u> is a model of the sphinx, a mythological creature with a human head and a lion's body.

INT
15. <u>Who</u> are the characters in *Death of a Salesman*?

DEM
16. <u>These</u> were the least expensive tools I could find.

INT
17. For <u>whom</u> did you write that song?

DEM
18. Whew! <u>That</u> was a near miss!

INT
19. <u>What</u> is the name of your younger brother?

DEM
20. <u>This</u> has been a popular tourist attraction for years.

The Pronoun C, pp. 7–8

EXERCISE A

1. The wallet <u>that is on the table</u> is mine.

2. This cactus, <u>which is quite large</u>, is native to Mexico and the states of Arizona and California.

3. Unfortunately, the car <u>that we bought last week</u> already has a large dent.

4. The person <u>who usually works the switchboard</u> is on vacation.

5. Ms. Ross, <u>whom I highly recommend</u>, is an outstanding piano teacher.

6. Strawberries, <u>which are Tom's favorite fruit</u>, are not in season right now.

7. Howard Hughes, <u>who amassed an enormous fortune over his lifetime</u>, spent much of his life in seclusion.

8. The old towels <u>that we use as rags</u> are in the cabinet.

9. In small businesses, the employee <u>who has the most seniority</u> is often given first consideration for promotion.

10. Our dog, <u>which is an Irish setter</u>, sleeps in the laundry room.

EXERCISE B

11. several
12. Everything
13. Neither
14. no one
15. Nothing

The Adjective, pp. 9–10

EXERCISE A

1. The restaurant offers a <u>wide</u> selection of <u>main</u> dishes and <u>free</u> refills of beverages.

2. The <u>highest</u> mountain in Washington, Mount Rainier is actually a <u>dormant</u> volcano.

3. Please order <u>fourteen</u> <u>new</u> stools for the <u>chemistry</u> lab.

4. Christopher Wren, a <u>prominent</u> architect of the 1600s, designed the <u>majestic</u> St. Paul's Cathedral in London.

5. Scientists have made <u>exciting</u> and <u>important</u> discoveries about dinosaurs.

6. Did Michael make the <u>oak</u> bookshelves in the <u>front</u> hallway?

7. Grandmother's recipe for <u>banana nut</u> bread requires <u>two</u> cups of <u>mashed</u> bananas.

8. Rabbits and hares have <u>long</u> ears and <u>long hind</u> legs.

9. The flight attendants were <u>helpful</u>, <u>knowledgeable</u>, and <u>courteous</u>.

10. Last night, the <u>full</u> moon was <u>beautiful</u>.

EXERCISE B

11. We searched <u>several</u> databases but found <u>little</u> <u>useful</u> information for the project.

12. Plutonium is a <u>radioactive chemical</u> element.

13. The divers were <u>happy</u> when they found the <u>sunken</u> ship.

14. The <u>sports</u> competition required participants to invent a <u>new</u> game using <u>old</u> equipment.

15. Marie, talented and dedicated, contributed to the literary magazine.

16. These pearls are synthetic.

17. Cliff crafted a large wooden table that will fit on the porch.

18. An urgent matter requires immediate attention.

19. May I borrow the blue pen and a clean sheet of paper?

20. Though the plant appears delicate, it is quite hardy.

The Verb A, pp. 11–12

EXERCISE A

1. Pumpkins should be harvested in the fall.

2. Todd often has taught community education classes.

3. Did Thomas Jefferson negotiate the Louisiana Purchase with France?

4. The box office will open at nine.

5. How does a water clock measure time?

6. He shall arrive soon after the press corps.

7. Jeannine has typed a résumé and scheduled several job interviews.

8. Mark and Debbie will grind their own wheat for bread.

9. Perhaps we should have been paying closer attention to the time.

10. Janice must have stumbled over that branch on the sidewalk.

EXERCISE B

11. How did early Native Americans shape and hollow out logs for dugouts, a type of canoe?

12. The committee isn't allotting any more money for research this year.

13. Have you read *The Marble Faun* by Nathaniel Hawthorne?

14. She is hoping for a postcard from her grandparents.

15. In ten minutes, that puppy will have been barking for two hours.

16. Will they be renting an apartment or buying a house?

17. Isn't that picture leaning a little bit to the left?

18. The term *holly* can be applied to over four hundred species of red- or black-berried plants.

19. Hadn't the teacher assigned homework for this weekend?

20. This dish may be served either hot or cold.

The Verb B, pp. 13–14

EXERCISE A

1. remembered

2. printed

3. initial, sign

4. climbed

5. constructed

6. recalls

7. builds, collects

8. ambled, ate

9. erupted

10. illuminate

EXERCISE B

11. LINK

12. ACT

13. ACT

14. ACT

15. LINK

16. LINK

17. ACT

18. ACT

19. LINK

20. LINK

The Verb C, pp. 15–16
EXERCISE A
1. Does Carol have a copy of the notes from history class?
2. Beverly Sills began her career as an opera singer at age eighteen.
3. The birds gathered dry grass and tufts of dog hair for their nests.
4. Has Frederick finished his homework yet?
5. An impressive structure, the Sears Tower in Chicago has 110 floors.
6. The copy machine needs toner and paper.
7. Felicia chooses her vehicles for their safety features and style.
8. Will you be sending the package first class?
9. The Mughal emperor Shah Jahan built the Taj Mahal in honor of his wife.
10. That company awards scholarships to children of employees.

EXERCISE B
11. TRANS
12. INT
13. INT
14. TRANS
15. TRANS
16. INT
17. TRANS
18. INT
19. TRANS
20. TRANS

The Adverb, pp. 17–18
EXERCISE A
1. The superintendent dealt with the situation fairly.
2. During the trial, the attorney presented her case effectively.
3. My hiking boots were completely covered with mud.
4. I looked everywhere for the lost library book.
5. American folklorist Carl Sandburg wrote poetically about the strength of people.

EXERCISE B
6. The virus is entirely new, and researchers are trying to understand how it spreads.
7. Karl Marx's socialist philosophies were quite controversial in many circles.
8. The students, unusually attentive during the presentation, applauded when the lecture ended.
9. The hundred-year-old house was in remarkably good condition.
10. The special effects in the film are truly amazing.

EXERCISE C
11. Only rarely have sailors spotted giant squid.
12. Our cousins arrived too late for the first song.
13. After a strong gust of wind, paper and leaves were scattered nearly everywhere.
14. We entered the dark cave somewhat reluctantly.
15. Although she feels nervous in a crisis, Sandra reacts quite calmly.

The Preposition, pp. 19–20
EXERCISE A
1. Before his career with the Yankees, baseball great Lou Gehrig attended Columbia University.
2. We rode the elevator to the top of the Empire State Building.

3. With no moving <u>parts</u>, solar cells are an ideal power supply <u>in</u> <u>space</u>.

4. Ms. Stapleton brought us a basket <u>of</u> <u>vegetables</u> <u>from</u> her <u>garden</u>.

5. All <u>of</u> the <u>tools</u> are <u>in</u> the <u>garage</u>.

6. The commission has changed its strategy <u>for</u> the <u>future</u>.

7. My cat's favorite toy is a sock filled <u>with</u> <u>catnip</u>.

8. The park ranger walked slowly <u>toward</u> the bear <u>cub</u>.

9. <u>Near</u> the subway <u>station</u> there's an old newspaper stand.

10. Nearly 80 percent <u>of</u> the <u>shipment</u> was damaged <u>by</u> the <u>storm</u>.

EXERCISE B

11. ADV
12. PREP
13. ADV
14. PREP
15. PREP

The Conjunction and the Interjection, pp. 21–22

EXERCISE A

1. so
2. but
3. not only . . . but also
4. Neither . . . nor
5. and

EXERCISE B

6. <u>If</u> we hurry, we'll miss the traffic.

7. Ethan took a detour <u>because</u> the main road was closed.

8. <u>Unless</u> the outfit goes on sale, I will not buy it.

9. <u>Though</u> the refrigerator was somewhat expensive, it should last for a long time.

10. We printed extra copies <u>so that</u> we would have enough for everyone.

EXERCISE C

<u>strong</u> 11. <u>Aha</u>! The mystery is solved!

<u>strong</u> 12. <u>Whew</u>! That was a close call!

<u>mild</u> 13. <u>Well</u>, there's always next season.

<u>mild</u> 14. <u>Ah</u>, isn't the warm ocean breeze relaxing?

<u>strong</u> 15. <u>Hey</u>! That dog is running away with the newspaper!

Chapter 2: Parts of a Sentence
pp. 23–34

Subjects, pp. 23–24

EXERCISE A

1. Two of the judges agreed to hear the case.

2. Glowing brightly against the night sky was the light from the old lighthouse.

3. Are all of the autographs authentic?

4. Here are the plans for the new addition to the house.

5. The chemists were wearing safety glasses and protective clothing.

6. At the end of the street lives a family from the Netherlands.

7. Was that map created by a famous explorer?

8. Members of the club will meet next Friday at four o'clock.

9. Pittsburgh was built at the intersection of two rivers that become the Ohio River.

10. Did everyone at the reception sign the guest book?

EXERCISE B

11. Did Cecilia or Lawrence find Ms. Clay's car keys?

12. Haiku and tanka are both forms of Japanese poetry.

13. At the career fair, an oceanographer, an actor, and a cartoonist gave the most interesting presentations.

14. Sopranos, altos, tenors, and basses sing together in our community choir.

15. Exceptional hitters, Hank Aaron and Ty Cobb set many records in professional baseball.

Predicates, pp. 25–26

EXERCISE A

1. Has the game schedule been posted on the bulletin board?

2. A Norse explorer, Leif Ericson is often considered the first European on North American shores.

3. During peak traffic hours, we usually ride the subway.

4. During the night, a gust of wind blew a large branch onto the roof of the house.

5. Will the Russian ballet company perform at the local theater this weekend?

6. Most folk songs have survived through an oral tradition rather than a written one.

7. Ralph, the winner of the door prize, presented his ticket to the store manager.

8. Does the manufacturer's warranty cover labor costs?

9. Kung fu, a martial art, combines exercise with concentration and self-discipline.

10. Should the government preserve more land for national parks?

EXERCISE B

11. Did anyone call or leave a message for me today?

12. A noted scientist, Alfred Nobel invented dynamite and founded the Nobel Prizes.

13. Should we recycle these boxes or store them in the attic?

14. As his first project, Val sanded the wood and primed it.

15. During autumn, leaves turn bright colors and fall from the trees.

Direct Objects, pp. 27–28

EXERCISE A

1. I need some <u>film</u> and a new <u>battery</u> for my camera.

2. Has the rain washed the <u>mud</u> off the sidewalk?

3. The famous architect Frank Lloyd Wright popularized certain home <u>designs</u> in the twentieth century.

4. They pitched their <u>tents</u> close to the lake.

5. The actor performed an amazing <u>stunt</u>!

6. Haven't you already received <u>information</u> and an <u>application</u>?

7. For the quilt, Sidney arranged the <u>strips</u> of fabric in a "log cabin" pattern.

8. An early advocate for women's rights, Mary Wollstonecraft wrote <u>*A Vindication of the Rights of Woman*</u> in 1792.

9. After the yard sale, Chandra will donate <u>whatever is left</u> to the thrift store.

10. The English sport of rugby requires an oval <u>ball</u> similar to an American football.

EXERCISE B

11. The gardener clipped the hedges <u>straight</u> and <u>even</u>.

12. City employees decorated the city hall <u>red</u>, <u>white</u>, and <u>blue</u> in honor of Independence Day.

13. Does the Food and Drug Administration consider these chemicals <u>safe</u>?

14. The Morrises named their children <u>Ramón</u> and <u>Isabel</u>.

15. You have made our visit <u>pleasant</u>!

Indirect Objects, pp. 29–30

EXERCISE A

1. A guest artist taught the <u>class</u> a lesson on perspective art.

2. Through much of history, parents awarded <u>whichever son was born first</u> most of the family's property.

3. The new store owner handed the first several <u>customers</u> gift certificates.

4. At the end of our baseball season, the former champions present the new <u>champions</u> the trophy.

5. Before a car leaves the factory, employees give <u>it</u> a thorough inspection.

6. Would you please save <u>me</u> a seat in the front row?

7. Juanita's teacher wrote <u>her</u> an excellent letter of recommendation.

8. King George V gave his <u>son</u> a home called Fort Belvedere.

9. The auctioneer sold the <u>buyers</u> the rest of the cars from the lot.

10. The mayor's presence lent the <u>event</u> an air of formality.

EXERCISE B *Answers to items 13 and 16 may vary.*

11. According to legend, a Greek soldier ran from Marathon to Athens and delivered the <u>citizens</u> <u>news</u> of an Athenian military victory.

12. The judges will present <u>whoever finishes first</u> and <u>whoever makes a perfect score</u> blue <u>ribbons</u>.

13. During baseball practice, the coach hit the <u>players</u> several ground <u>balls</u>.

14. Did you give <u>Jenny</u> and <u>Ted</u> <u>directions</u> to the house?

15. Did the Egyptian queen Cleopatra pledge Marc Antony her loyalty?

16. Every evening, Mr. Shelton reads his children a bedtime story.

17. My mother knitted my sister and me wool sweaters.

18. Has the teacher allowed Stan and Ian extra time for their reports?

19. Show Lori and Dale your wildlife sketches.

20. The supervisor assigned Gail and Shane the first two projects.

Predicate Nominatives, pp. 31–32

EXERCISE A

1. The purpose of the press conference was to clarify the senator's position on the issue.

2. For over a thousand years, Kyoto was the capital of Japan.

3. With his coach's encouragement, Evan has become a competitive swimmer.

4. Aren't the Burnetts good friends of yours?

5. What an entertaining speaker he is!

6. My parents are active volunteers in several service organizations.

7. Idaho did not become a state until 1890.

8. Charles will remain vice president until the end of March.

9. *The Federalist* papers were essays in support of the U.S. Constitution.

10. Gloves and a scarf are what I put on in cold weather.

EXERCISE B

Answers to items 11 and 17 may vary.

11. The only businesses in the neighborhood are the corner market and a small convenience store.

12. Two of my favorite paintings are the *Mona Lisa* and *The Starry Night*.

13. Mr. Carson's favorite types of programs are sports events and nature shows.

14. Two of the smallest countries in the Europe are Luxembourg and Belgium.

15. The first guests at the reception were Cheryl and I.

16. A pioneer in higher education for women, Mary Lyon was the founder and first principal of Mount Holyoke Female Seminary.

17. Did Tyrone become a computer programmer or a psychologist?

18. The earliest of Jane Austen's novels were *Sense and Sensibility* and *Pride and Prejudice*.

19. After a successful singing career, Sonny Bono became a mayor and later a U.S. representative.

20. The assistant band directors are Ms. Lawson and Mr. Samuelson.

Predicate Adjectives, pp. 33–34

EXERCISE A

1. The fresh blueberries were delicious in my oatmeal.

2. The air always smells fresh after a summer shower.

3. The crowd became restless in the third quarter.

4. Even in a hot desert, temperatures can turn cold at night.

5. After the meeting, everyone seemed confident about the chairperson's budget proposal.

6. Is this table narrow enough for the space beside the couch?

7. After learning more about chess, Nancy became more <u>enthusiastic</u> about the game.

8. <u>Powerful</u> were the speeches of Dr. Martin Luther King, Jr.

9. The novels of French writer and political activist Émile Zola were often <u>controversial</u>.

10. Does this outfit seem <u>appropriate</u> for the wedding reception?

EXERCISE B

11. Were your grandmother's parents <u>Puerto Rican</u> or <u>Italian</u>?

12. The holidays were <u>brief</u> but <u>restful</u>.

13. During the debate, both teams remained <u>calm</u> and <u>attentive</u>.

14. The old house looks <u>fresh</u> and <u>bright</u> in its new coat of paint.

15. The Guggenheim Museum's art collection is <u>extensive</u> and <u>diverse</u>.

16. <u>Thorough</u> and <u>informative</u> were Dr. Jacobson's lectures on genetics.

17. The personnel at the hospital are always <u>compassionate</u> and <u>sympathetic</u>.

18. Sometimes the moon appears <u>yellow</u> or even <u>orange</u> in the night sky.

19. <u>Cautious</u> and <u>deliberate</u> were the scientists during the dinosaur fossil's excavation.

20. This type of essay is <u>argumentative</u> or <u>persuasive</u>.

Chapter 3: The Phrase, pp. 35–44
The Prepositional Phrase, pp. 35–36
EXERCISE A

1. Water the plants on the back patio every day.
2. Next, we'll paint the shelves next to the stove.
3. Does the cat with the stripes needs its shots?
4. Trees near rivers usually have a good water supply.
5. The children behind the stage curtain practiced their lines once again.

EXERCISE B

6. Tim poured turpentine on the paintbrush.
7. Coach Winters wears her whistle during basketball games.
8. My grandmother, active in volunteer organizations, is often quite busy.
9. Dash to the front door and unlock it.
10. The old moose moved quickly for its age.

The Participle and the Participial Phrase, pp. 37–38
EXERCISE A

1. The balanced rock was precisely perched on the cliff's edge.
2. Quick! Get out of this pouring rain!
3. Laughing, the children played tag in the park.
4. Everyone's attention was on the ringing phone.
5. Did you see that well-researched report on the news last night?

EXERCISE B

6. Plugging in the toaster, Marsha wondered if there were any bagels.
7. The travelers, arriving at the airport in the nick of time, sighed with relief.

8. How long will the meeting rescheduled for this afternoon last?
9. Pushing snow to either side of the road, the snowplows pressed on.
10. The fan, bought at a flea market, did little to cool the room.

EXERCISE C

11. puffing
12. forcing
13. blown
14. laughing
15. Tapping

The Gerund and the Gerund Phrase, pp. 39–40
EXERCISE A

1. V
2. G
3. P
4. G
5. G
6. G
7. V
8. G
9. G
10. P

EXERCISE B

11. Nell is practicing her math by memorizing geometry theorems.
12. Measuring carefully is important in carpentry.
13. The dog enjoys chewing on the twigs from the pecan tree.
14. Raising livestock is hard work.
15. This crab moves by scuttling sideways.
16. Let's go dancing at that new club.
17. Running a marathon takes months of preparation.
18. Don't make the mistake of promising what you can't deliver.
19. Feeding the fish is one of Josh's daily chores.
20. He gives winning the match his full attention.

The Infinitive and the Infinitive Phrase, pp. 41–42

EXERCISE A

1. In front of the fireplace is a warm place <u>to sit</u>.

2. After a good performance, it's polite <u>to applaud</u>.

3. The tired child managed <u>to smile</u>.

4. <u>To finish</u> is my only concern at this point!

5. On a warm, breezy day, it's fun <u>to sail</u>.

6. Shane told us that he had finally learned <u>to draw</u>.

7. <u>To win</u> tonight would really improve the team's record.

8. The best course <u>to take</u> is the one proposed by the commission.

9. Once the water began filling the canoe, it began <u>to sink</u>.

10. This pair of slacks is sure <u>to fit</u>.

EXERCISE B

11. Thunder began <u>to boom loudly</u>.

12. Do you have anything <u>to say about this situation</u>?

13. <u>To lose herself in a good mystery novel</u> is Gina's wish right now.

14. <u>To reach the harbor</u>, turn right at the light and drive two miles.

15. Has Kayla ever been tempted <u>to tell your secret</u>?

16. You need <u>to lift this barbell slowly and steadily ten times</u>.

17. How <u>to cross the river safely</u> was the question.

18. It's important <u>to be really honest with your friends</u>.

19. The next step is <u>to ventilate the room thoroughly</u>.

20. <u>To resolve this issue permanently</u> will require time and effort.

The Appositive and the Appositive Phrase, pp. 43–44

EXERCISE A

1. That man, <u>Dr. Nathan Bedford</u>, has already testified in court.

2. This book, <u>Walden</u>, is a favorite in our English class.

3. Which boy is your brother <u>Jason</u>?

4. That store, <u>Dollar-and-Dime</u>, sells paper goods and other items.

5. Do you play her favorite instrument, <u>guitar</u>?

6. This Thursday, we <u>volunteers</u> will begin our final fundraising campaign.

7. The museum's latest acquisitions, <u>sculptures</u>, are now on display.

8. One of her friends, <u>Jerome</u>, will be helping us build the float.

9. The yard sale begins tomorrow, <u>Wednesday</u>, unless it rains.

10. The dog is learning a new skill, <u>obedience</u>.

EXERCISE B

11. Flour, <u>an important ingredient in baking</u>, comes in several varieties.

12. Sit and watch this show, <u>a suspenseful science fiction drama</u>, with me.

13. <u>A chore I don't mind at all</u>, mowing the lawn actually relaxes me.

14. The long train, <u>loaded freight cars and beat-up box cars</u>, blocked traffic for at least ten minutes.

15. Ficus, <u>tropical plants with shiny leaves</u>, are sometimes grown as ornamentals.

16. Beaches and ski slopes, <u>popular vacation destinations</u>, are always crowded in season.

17. The clean laundry, <u>freshly washed jeans and socks</u>, lay stacked on the kitchen table.

18. Hawks and eagles, <u>both birds of prey</u>, have hook-tipped beaks.

19. The advisor, <u>attorney Mavis Newton of Dallas</u>, is an expert in medical legal issues.

20. The clouds, <u>streaks of pink against the sky</u>, reflected the sunset.

Chapter 4: The Clause, pp. 45–54

The Adjective Clause, pp. 45–46

EXERCISE A

1. Please wind the (clock) that sits on the mantel.

2. Is the Scott family looking for a (car) that has lots of legroom?

3. The (chairperson), to whom the committee listened closely, outlined the proposal.

4. Where is the (trophy) that Samantha won at the tennis match?

5. Do you remember the (time) when Aunt Emma taught us to fish?

EXERCISE B

_NE_ 6. Many kindergarten teachers keep healthful snacks handy for their students, who get hungry often.

_E_ 7. On the bulletin board, the teacher displayed art that the children had made.

_NE_ 8. Letters and numbers, which are the building blocks of writing and math, are taught to these children.

_NE_ 9. The children also play finger games, which improve motor skills and hand-eye coordination.

_E_ 10. Their teachers must be people who enjoy the company of small children.

_NE_ 11. My best friend, whom I've known since kindergarten, is in my math class.

_E_ 12. Is that the book that you've been looking for?

_E_ 13. Those pictures remind me of a time when I didn't worry about anything.

_E_ 14. Isn't the site where the old elementary school stood being turned into a park?

_NE_ 15. The new elementary school, which my youngest brother will attend, was just completed last year.

The Noun Clause, pp. 47–48

EXERCISE A

1. IO
2. DO
3. PN
4. S
5. OP

EXERCISE B

6. Only his mother knew why the child was laughing.

7. Where the treasure is buried remains a mystery to this very day.

8. Will each student conduct an interview with whoever has inspired him or her?

9. The final decision is whether we should travel by car or by train.

10. Notify whichever teacher is closest if a problem occurs.

EXERCISE C

_PN_ 11. Careful consideration is what is required now.

_DO_ 12. Kevin asked when the movie starts.

_OP_ 13. Let's get in line at whichever cash register has the fewest people waiting.

_PN_ **14.** The stadium is <u>where all the</u> <u>excitement is happening</u>.

_S_ **15.** <u>That the kitten attacked its own</u> <u>reflection</u> amused all of us.

The Adverb Clause, pp. 49–50

EXERCISE A

1. <u>As long as Michelle keeps practicing</u>, her abilities <u>will grow</u>.

2. <u>Relieved because the hard rain had</u> <u>stopped</u>, Nicholas steered the car back out onto the road.

3. Please <u>continue</u> working on the test <u>until</u> <u>time is called</u>.

4. <u>Since the store's inventory sold more</u> <u>quickly than expected</u>, employees <u>may go</u> home early.

5. <u>When the curtain had risen completely</u>, Susan <u>walked</u> onto the stage.

EXERCISE B

6. George <u>should study</u> anatomy carefully <u>if he wants to be a personal trainer for</u> <u>athletes</u>.

7. <u>Will</u> Nell <u>help</u> her brother with his homework <u>so that he will complete it on</u> <u>time</u>?

8. Sam must kick the ball <u>harder</u> <u>than he has</u> <u>so far</u>, or he will not be able to score.

9. Please <u>put</u> another coat of paint on the wall <u>because the old color is showing through</u>.

10. <u>When we take our dog Pepper to the dog</u> <u>park</u>, she always <u>comes</u> home tired but happy.

EXERCISE C

11. <u>When building a campfire</u>, start with small pieces of dry wood.

12. Adrienne sings more loudly <u>than Janet</u>.

13. The painter carefully mixed new paint <u>while waiting for the canvas to dry</u>.

14. <u>When revising their writing</u>, some students choose to read aloud to a friend.

15. Marta received as many notes of congratulations <u>as her sister</u>.

Sentence Structure A, pp. 51–52

EXERCISE A

1. <u>Hal</u> and <u>I</u> <u>carve</u> wood into sculptures.

2. Some <u>people</u> <u>prefer</u> quieter hobbies.

3. For example, my <u>brother</u> <u>spends</u> many hours watching birds.

4. <u>Did</u> <u>he</u> <u>see</u> a new species of bird for the first time yesterday?

5. Almost <u>everyone</u> <u>has</u> some sort of hobby or <u>collects</u> something.

EXERCISE B

_S_ **6.** It took only minutes to douse the fire completely.

_C_ **7.** <u>Not even an ember glowed in the</u> <u>ashes</u>; <u>as a result, the stars seemed to</u> <u>shine more brightly than before</u>.

_C_ **8.** <u>The campers looked at the stars in</u> <u>awe</u>; <u>after all, most of the boys were</u> <u>used to bright city lights and dim</u> <u>stars</u>.

_S_ **9.** <u>In the distance, a coyote yowled</u>, <u>paused, and then yipped</u>.

_C_ **10.** <u>The campers called goodnight to one</u> <u>another</u>; <u>then they zipped their tents</u> <u>up and slept</u>.

EXERCISE C

11. C

12. C

13. S

14. C

15. S

EXERCISE A

1. Composers spend time composing catchy jingles so that people will walk around whistling and humming them.

2. Because the images in ads are so important, sometimes there are no words at all.

3. Although there are quiet ads, many ads scream at viewers to get their attention.

4. Have you ever enjoyed an ad but forgotten what product it was for right away?

5. Because so many people watch the Super Bowl, it costs millions of dollars to run an ad during that event.

EXERCISE B

__Cx__ 6. Some people like to read history, while others prefer romance.

__Cd-Cx__ 7. Have you ever been swept up in a book, even though you knew it was only a story, and have you ever been sorry when you reached the last page?

__Cd-Cx__ 8. Magazines, which cover every possible interest, have many readers as well; in fact, our family currently subscribes to seven magazines because everyone in the family wants to read something different.

__Cx__ 9. If you want to keep up with the daily news, there's still no beating a good city newspaper, which has coverage of local, national, and global events and issues.

__Cd-Cx__ 10. However, some people like to get their news from the Internet, or they listen to news radio programs while they do chores around the house.

Subject-Verb Agreement A, pp. 55–56

EXERCISE A

1. Many <u>industries</u> (*rely, relies*) on the work of robots.

2. For example, the automotive <u>industry</u> (*uses, use*) robots on assembly lines.

3. Certain <u>robots</u> (*welds, weld*) vehicle bodies.

4. At a different stage of the process, another <u>robot</u> (*paints, paint*) the vehicles.

5. (*Do, Does*) an <u>engineer</u> design a different robot for each specific task?

EXERCISE B

6. (*Does, Do*) the <u>president</u> and the <u>vice-president</u> meet each day?

7. The <u>refrigerator</u>, the <u>dishwasher</u>, or the <u>disposal</u> (*hum, hums*) rather loudly.

8. <u>Leon</u> and <u>Lana</u> (*love, loves*) being on the debate team.

9. Neither the <u>planet</u> nor its <u>moon</u> (*sustain, sustains*) life.

10. In their jobs, <u>lawyers</u> and <u>politicians</u> (*debates, debate*) many issues.

11. After high school <u>he</u> and <u>I</u> (*am, are*) going to college.

12. The <u>chairs</u> or the <u>coffee table</u> (*fit, fits*) next to the sofa.

13. (*Has, Have*) <u>you</u> and <u>she</u> chosen careers in the legal profession?

14. The <u>principal</u> or the <u>teachers</u> (*counts, count*) the votes.

15. <u>Rachel</u>, <u>Phil</u>, or the <u>editor</u> (*writes, write*) about every election.

Subject-Verb Agreement B, pp. 57–58

EXERCISE A

1. Strange <u>lights</u> across the lake (*flashes, flash*) along the shore every night.

2. Each morning, a delivery <u>truck</u> that carries packages (*stops, stop*) at the corner.

3. A <u>banana</u>, together with those berries, (*makes, make*) a tasty smoothie.

4. The <u>artists</u> who own this studio (*has, have*) filled it with their own art.

5. His <u>property</u>, which includes a house and a barn, (*is, are*) for sale.

EXERCISE B

6. After lunch <u>someone</u> always (*feeds, feed*) the parakeet.

7. (*Is, Are*) <u>many</u> in the stands cheering for my brother?

8. (*Has, Have*) <u>anybody</u> seen my beach towel and sunscreen lotion?

9. <u>One</u> of the scientists (*have, has*) discovered a new vaccine.

10. At the same moment, <u>both</u> (*jumps, jump*) for the basketball.

11. Once underwater, <u>each</u> quickly (*swim, swims*) toward the school of fish.

12. (*Is, Are*) <u>something</u> in that large blue bag for you?

13. Luckily, <u>nothing</u> on that buffet table (*tempt, tempts*) me to overeat tonight.

14. Every evening, <u>several</u> (*gather, gathers*) near the edge of the clearing.

15. <u>Neither</u> (*run, runs*) faster than that little bird can fly.

EXERCISE C

16. <u>Most</u> of the movie (*has, have*) been very suspenseful.

17. (*Are, Is*) <u>any</u> of the apartments on the list already furnished?

18. <u>More</u> of the proposals under discussion (*sound, sounds*) sensible now.

19. <u>None</u> of the other players (*score, scores*) as well as Rosa.

20. By the end of the game, <u>all</u> of his uniform (*was, were*) drenched with sweat.

Subject-Verb Agreement C, pp. 59–60

EXERCISE A

1. doesn't
2. Is
3. Don't
4. lives
5. fly
6. don't
7. bring
8. recruits
9. don't
10. Was

EXERCISE B

11. is
12. Does
13. were
14. live
15. was

Subject-Verb Agreement D, pp. 61–62

EXERCISE A

1. (*Is, Are*) <u>mathematics</u> your favorite subject in school?

2. For durability, the <u>eyeglasses</u> (*has, have*) spring-loaded hinges.

3. According to Aunt Leigh, <u>molasses</u> (*adds, add*) a good flavor to bread.

4. Usually, the local <u>news</u> (*features, feature*) at least one human-interest story.

5. <u>Binoculars</u> (*magnifies, magnify*) an object in the distance.

EXERCISE B

6. shares
7. C
8. tells
9. has
10. Does

EXERCISE C

11. was
12. is
13. were
14. are
15. were

Pronoun-Antecedent Agreement A, pp. 63–64

EXERCISE A

1. its
2. their
3. his
4. her
5. their

EXERCISE B

6. On summer days <u>Michelle</u> and <u>Felicia</u> spend (*her, their*) afternoons together.

7. <u>Ella</u> or <u>Sue Ann</u> will bring an ice chest full of cold fruit drinks with (*her, them*).

8. Neither the <u>deck</u> nor the <u>table</u> has (*its, their*) surface sealed against rain.

9. A <u>book</u>, a <u>magazine</u>, and good <u>food</u> provide (*its, their*) own kind of entertainment.

10. This <u>card</u> and that <u>envelope</u> have familiar handwriting on (*it, them*).

11. In the backyard a <u>tree</u> or an <u>umbrella</u> is useful because (*it, they*) provides shade.

12. <u>Dad</u> or <u>Joe</u> sometimes offers sandwiches when (*he, they*) makes lunch.

13. Often our <u>cat</u> and <u>dog</u> treat (*itself*, <u>*themselves*</u>) to a swim in our backyard pool.

14. Is <u>Ken</u> or <u>Vern</u> famous in the neighborhood for (<u>*his*</u>, *their*) "backyard banquets"?

15. Are the <u>books</u> and <u>magazines</u> in (*its*, <u>*their*</u>) usual place next to the reclining chair?

Pronoun-Antecedent Agreement B, pp. 65–66

EXERCISE A

1. her
2. his or her
3. him
4. himself or herself
5. it

EXERCISE B

6. Does <u>most</u> of the road to your house have asphalt on (<u>*its*</u>, *their*) surface?

7. Chad talked with <u>both</u> of the mechanics about (*his or her*, <u>*their*</u>) estimates.

8. <u>Several</u> of the watches are broken. Can (*it*, <u>*they*</u>) be fixed?

9. <u>None</u> of the truck drivers are tired. Will (*he or she*, <u>*they*</u>) drive another hour?

10. <u>All</u> of the fence has been painted. Please don't touch (<u>*it*</u>, *them*).

EXERCISE C

11. it
12. her
13. its
14. them
15. its

Chapter 6: Using Pronouns Correctly, pp. 67–72

Personal Pronouns A, pp. 67–68

EXERCISE A

1. they
2. he
3. she
4. he
5. they
6. She
7. they
8. she
9. we
10. I

EXERCISE B

11. hers
12. yours
13. Your
14. mine
15. his

Personal Pronouns B, pp. 69–70

EXERCISE A

1. them
2. me
3. him
4. her
5. me
6. them
7. him
8. her
9. them
10. them

EXERCISE B

The strikethroughs are to help students choose the correct pronoun. They are not meant to be graded, though the teacher may require them.

11. That roller coaster ride is thrilling for ~~Justin and~~ (I, _me_).

12. When did Uncle Bart make ~~Holly and~~ (_them_, they) that tire swing?

13. Grandpa showed ~~the neighbors and~~ (_us_, we) some old photographs.

14. Will this secret stay between ~~you and~~ (I, _me_)?

15. Where did you find ~~Chi and~~ (_him_, he) those unusual Christmas gifts?

16. Coach McIntire sent ~~the pitcher and~~ (_her_, she) a secret signal.

17. Please give ~~Mr. Tatum or~~ (I, _me_) your permission slips for the field trip.

18. These plates of chicken and biscuits are for ~~you and~~ (they, _them_).

19. There was a safety railing between ~~the edge of the cliff and~~ (we, _us_).

20. I wish ~~you and~~ (she, _her_) many happy times together.

Special Problems in Pronoun Usage, pp. 71–72

EXERCISE A

1. she
2. We
3. them
4. us
5. him

EXERCISE B

6. Who
7. whom
8. who
9. who
10. Whom

Chapter 7: Clear Reference, pp. 73–76

Clear Pronoun Reference A, pp. 73–74

EXERCISE A

The arrows are to help students determine whether the reference is clear or ambiguous. Though the teacher may require the arrows, they are not meant to be graded.

  A   **1.** Megan met Sonia at the movies, and she offered to buy some popcorn.

  C   **2.** Wayne eats a nutritious snack before he baby-sits Tommy for the afternoon.

  A   **3.** When the bowling ball hit the pin, it fell into the gutter.

  A   **4.** When the teacher talks to the student, does he make eye contact?

  C   **5.** Greg repaired an old sailboat, and he went sailing yesterday.

EXERCISE B

Answers will vary. Sample answers are provided.

6. The tornado uprooted a tree near our house. That tornado really scared me.

7. When the leaves turn red, the trees look beautiful.

8. To my amusement, the cat suddenly pounced on the box.

9. The beautiful horses raced around the field.

10. Did Melanie find Amy in the mall? Did Amy have the car keys?

Clear Pronoun Reference B, pp. 75–76

EXERCISE A

The arrow is to help students determine whether the reference is clear or weak. Though the teacher may require the arrow, it is not meant to be graded.

  W   **1.** Jennifer enrolled in the journalism class because she wants to be a professional one.

  W   **2.** Although I believe that friends should be honest with each other, it is not always easy.

  W   **3.** Did Grace open her sister's closet and try several on?

  C   **4.** The statistics surprised the professor. Are they accurate?

  W   **5.** I couldn't make photocopies of the worksheets because it was out of order.

EXERCISE B

Answers may vary. Sample answers are provided.

6. In the army, soldiers learn discipline, stamina, and obedience.

7. My grandparents own a bakery, and they make their baked goods fresh every morning.

8. Find the number for the fire department! We need firefighters now!

9. The comic strip shows an argument between Charlie Brown and Lucy.

10. The class spent several hours in the museum and studied one sculpture in particular.

Chapter 8: Using Verbs Correctly, pp. 77–92

Principal Parts of Verbs A, pp. 77–78

EXERCISE A

1. present participle
2. past participle
3. base form
4. past
5. past participle
6. base form
7. present participle
8. past
9. past participle
10. present participle

EXERCISE B

11. print [is] _printing_ _printed_ [have] _printed_
12. _propose_ [is] _proposing_ proposed [have] _proposed_
13. _chase_ [is] _chasing_ _chased_ [have] _chased_
14. _giggle_ [is] _giggling_ giggled [have] _giggled_
15. borrow [is] _borrowing_ _borrowed_ [have] _borrowed_
16. snare [is] _snaring_ _snared_ [have] _snared_
17. _unpack_ [is] _unpacking_ _unpacked_ [have] unpacked
18. stop [is] _stopping_ _stopped_ [have] _stopped_
19. _dribble_ [is] dribbling _dribbled_ [have] _dribbled_
20. call [is] _calling_ _called_ [have] _called_

Principal Parts of Verbs B, pp. 79–80

EXERCISE A

1. _sink_ [is] _sinking_ _sank_ [have] sunk
2. _take_ [is] _taking_ took [have] _taken_
3. cost [is] _costing_ _cost_ [have] _cost_
4. _tear_ [is] _tearing_ torn [have] _torn_
5. _lose_ [is] losing _lost_ [have] _lost_
6. sing [is] _singing_ _sang_ [have] _sung_
7. _eat_ [is] _eating_ _ate_ [have] eaten
8. _set_ [is] _setting_ set [have] _set_
9. hide [is] _hiding_ _hid_ [have] _hidden_
10. _spend_ [is] spending _spent_ [have] _spent_

EXERCISE B

11. come
12. burst
13. woke
14. stolen
15. have rung

Lie and *Lay, Sit* and *Set, Rise* and *Raise,* pp. 81–82

EXERCISE A

1. lay; laid
2. lay; lie
3. laid; lain
4. lying; lay
5. lay; lying

EXERCISE B

6. sets; sit
7. sitting; set
8. set; sat
9. sitting; sitting
10. sit; set

EXERCISE C

11. raise; rise
12. rose; raised
13. rising; raising
14. raised; rose
15. risen; raised

Tense, pp. 83–84

EXERCISE A

1. future
2. present
3. past perfect
4. past
5. present perfect
6. present
7. present perfect
8. future perfect
9. past
10. future

EXERCISE B

11. believed
12. will believe
13. have believed
14. believe
15. will have believed

16. studied
17. will study
18. have studied
19. had studied
20. will have studied

Progressive Forms of Verbs, pp. 85–86

EXERCISE A

1. was performing
2. will be painting
3. was ringing
4. is crawling
5. was playing

EXERCISE B

6. had been learning
7. have been paving
8. will have been migrating
9. will have been living
10. had been saving

EXERCISE C

11. future perfect progressive
12. present perfect progressive
13. present progressive
14. past progressive
15. future progressive

The Uses of Tenses, pp. 87–88

EXERCISE A

1. present
2. present
3. past
4. future
5. past

EXERCISE B

6. present perfect
7. future perfect
8. past perfect
9. future perfect
10. present perfect

EXERCISE A

1. retreated
2. will go
3. did
4. maintains
5. has returned

EXERCISE B

6. will go
7. had
8. composed
9. returned
10. had

EXERCISE C

Except for item 12, answers will vary. Sample student responses are provided.

___I___ 11. Grandma promised that she and Grandpa <s>visited</s> *will visit* us next Sunday.

___C___ 12. Lola had discovered her love of music long before she joined the band.

___I___ 13. The pond <s>is</s> *was* rising while the rain fell.

___I___ 14. As a child, Kevin watched television programs in Spanish, and he <s>will learn</s> *learned* the language from those programs.

___I___ 15. Has everyone decided what he or she <s>orders</s> *will order* from the menu?

Active Voice and Passive Voice, pp. 91–92

EXERCISE A

1. P
2. P
3. A
4. A
5. P
6. P
7. P
8. A
9. P
10. A

EXERCISE B

Answers may vary. Sample student responses are provided.

11. Yesterday, new locks were installed by a skilled locksmith.
    Yesterday, a skilled locksmith installed new locks.

12. The traffic accident will be investigated.
    This sentence should remain in the passive voice because we don't know who performs the action.

13. Last Sunday, our fantastic dinner was prepared by me.
    Last Sunday, I prepared our fantastic dinner.

14. All stockholders have been sent their dividends.
    This sentence should remain in the passive voice to emphasize the receiver of the action.

15. Unfortunately, a lie about what happened was told by someone.
    Unfortunately, someone told a lie about what happened.

Chapter 9: Using Modifiers Correctly, pp. 93–100

Troublesome Modifiers A, pp. 93–94

EXERCISE A

1. bad
2. badly
3. badly
4. bad
5. badly
6. bad
7. bad
8. badly
9. bad
10. bad

EXERCISE B

11. well
12. good
13. well
14. good
15. good
16. good
17. good
18. well
19. well
20. good

Troublesome Modifiers B, pp. 95–96

EXERCISE A

1. really
2. real
3. really
4. real
5. really
6. really
7. really
8. real
9. really
10. real

EXERCISE B

11. slowly
12. slow
13. slow
14. Slowly
15. slowly
16. slow
17. slowly
18. slow
19. slow
20. slowly

Degrees of Comparison, pp. 97–98

EXERCISE A

1. less expensive
2. funniest
3. more rapidly
4. less interesting
5. most outrageous
6. less noisy
7. lightest
8. less softly
9. least fearsome
10. more colorful

EXERCISE B

11. more
12. most
13. better
14. best
15. worse

Uses of Comparisons, pp. 99–100

EXERCISE A

1. My dog Fido learned the commands more quickly than any *other* dog in the class.
2. The grass is ~~greenest~~ *greener* on the other side of the fence.
3. I've put together over fifty jigsaw puzzles, and this one is the ~~more~~ *most* difficult.
4. C
5. Of the two parrots, this one is ~~most~~ *more* colorful.

6. I considered yellow, blue, or green paint for my bedroom. I liked yellow best.

7. Which play did you enjoy more, *Hamlet* or *The Taming of the Shrew*?

8. Tyrone collected more canned goods than anyone else in the class.

9. Carrying the couch up the stairs was more difficult than carrying the chairs up the stairs.

10. *C*

Answers may vary.

11. The computer monitors in the drafting lab are bigger than the monitors in the writing lab.

12. Of all the grocery stores near my home, the one on Fourth Street has the freshest produce.

13. *C*

14. During the camping trip, we swam, hiked, and canoed, and I liked hiking best.

15. Mrs. Fermo is the friendliest of the five board members.

Chapter 10: Placement of Modifiers, pp. 101–104

Placement of Modifiers A, pp. 101–102

EXERCISE A

Answers may vary. Sample answers are provided.

1. Delighted, the fireworks surprised the children.

2. I found the book in my room that was due yesterday.

3. The bicycle is in the shed with a flat tire.

4. Escaping, the boy tried to grab the tail of the kite.

5. Karen's soccer team is ranked second in the state; her team has nearly won all of its games.

6. Ringing, I ran for the phone.

7. The canoe slid through the water, built by hand.

8. We finished reading a short story written by Mark Twain during study hall.

9. Hundreds of pumpkins lay in the fields, which were almost ripe.

10. The supervisor complimented the carpenters for working so quickly as he handed out their paychecks.

EXERCISE B

11. S
12. C
13. S
14. S
15. C

Placement of Modifiers B, pp. 103–104

EXERCISE A

1. D
2. C
3. D
4. D
5. D
6. D
7. C
8. D
9. C
10. D

EXERCISE B

Answers will vary. Sample answers are provided. Red underscore indicates dangling modifier prior to revision.

11. While we watched the sun set over the ocean, the sky turned purple, red, and orange. (While watching the sun set over the ocean,)

12. Having run several miles, the members of the track team agreed that nothing is as refreshing as a cool glass of water.

13. After my brother and I baked bread, the house smelled wonderful! (After baking bread,)

14. Pestered by the flies buzzing around, the cow swatted its tail at them.

15. After completing the test, you should place the answer sheet inside the test booklet.

Chapter 11: A Glossary of Usage, pp. 105–12

Glossary of Usage A, pp. 105–106

EXERCISE A

1. accepted
2. all right
3. Except
4. affect
5. All right

EXERCISE B

6. A large number
7. backpack
8. somewhere
9. among
10. much
11. anyway
12. among
13. everywhere
14. between
15. is

Glossary of Usage B, pp. 107–108

EXERCISE A

1. Don't
2. done
3. doesn't
4. don't
5. done
6. did
7. doesn't
8. done
9. don't
10. done

EXERCISE B

11. taught
12. less
13. rather
14. Fewer
15. learned
16. fewer
17. teaches
18. fewer
19. somewhat
20. fewer

Glossary of Usage C, pp. 109–10

EXERCISE A

1. have
2. used
3. supposed
4. then
5. have
6. than
7. had
8. Then
9. supposed
10. than

EXERCISE B

11. who
12. try to
13. This
14. which
15. that
16. try to
17. that
18. this
19. that
20. try to

Glossary of Usage D, pp. 111–12

EXERCISE A

Answers will vary.

1. Don't you have ~~no~~ any manners?
2. My little sister ~~can't~~ can hardly talk yet.
3. Did hardly ~~no~~ any residents vote for the new property tax?
4. Couldn't Sarah find ~~no~~ any shoes she liked?
5. Don't ~~never~~ ever leave the car's engine running while you're at the gas pump!
6. Without a good light, I can't ~~barely~~ read comfortably.
7. There isn't ~~scarcely~~ time to finish the test.
8. I don't want ~~nothing~~ anything for dessert.

9. We ~~haven't~~ <u>have</u> bought scarcely enough flour for the recipe.

10. Permanent marker ~~shouldn't~~ <u>should</u> never be used on the white board.

Answers will vary.

11. My cousins Jack and Ann are training to become ~~airline stewards~~ <u>flight attendants</u>.

12. Ask the ~~deliveryman~~ <u>delivery person</u> to leave the package outside.

13. Mrs. Sims was elected president of that ~~businessmen's~~ <u>executives'</u> organization.

14. Is the material in this rug ~~man-made~~ <u>synthetic</u> or natural?

15. Aunt Deborah found a part-time job as a ~~watchman~~ <u>security guard</u> at the factory.

Chapter 12: Capitalization, pp.113–26

Capitalization A, pp. 113–14

EXERCISE A

1. Jessica said, "let's go out for lunch today."
2. our teacher was promoted to vice principal.
3. this computer runs slowly when the network is busy.
4. Alicia whispered, "when are the reports due?"
5. the cat stretched out its paw and swatted at the ball.
6. "where are we supposed to set these cases of juice?" asked Devon.
7. the spider has woven its web across the opening in the fence.
8. Grandma muttered, "well, I guess the bulb needs to be changed."
9. a mouse has been scratching around behind the walls of the storage shed.
10. Hey! there's a quarter lying next to the curb.

EXERCISE B

11. If you set the table, i'll wash the dishes tonight.
12. For the past two summers, i've volunteered at the animal shelter.
13. Jason and i rode our bicycles around Town Lake this weekend.
14. "This fall," Marta told us, "i'm going to visit my sister in Nevada."
15. I've decided that i should take the shuttle to the fairgrounds.

EXERCISE C

16. yours truly,
17. dear Aunt Teresa,
18. my darling Rebecca,
19. dear Professor Hanami:
20. sincerely yours,

Capitalization B, pp. 115–16

EXERCISE A

1. Will the company cookout be held at brentwood park?
2. My friend mario is playing center in tonight's basketball game.
3. Ms. samuels is making a speech to the committee.
4. I am visiting boston this summer.
5. Today's lecture is on the origin of arabic numerals.
6. One of the highest mountains in the world is nanga parbat.
7. Mr. Jesse and his dog once hiked across much of south carolina.
8. Doesn't a portuguese man-of-war have stinging cells in its tentacles?
9. That simple cabin was kentuckian Winslow Carter's birthplace.
10. The island of cuba gained its independence from Spain in 1898.

EXERCISE B

Answers will vary. Sample responses follow.

11. state   Florida
12. lake   Lake Travis
13. school   McNeil High School
14. team   Bradford Bears
15. month   December

16. her puppy Jack

17. Juanita F. Garcia

18. Francis Riggs, Jr.

19. Marcella L. Ward

20. my horse Barney

Capitalization C, pp. 117–18

EXERCISE A

1. Adam voted that we visit the grand canyon this year.

2. We made a map of argentina for geography class.

3. My friend Enrique lives in maine.

4. The new high school is on raines road.

5. The continent of europe is one of the smallest continents in the world.

6. Julia rode her bike around rosedale park.

7. A series of earthquakes began near mount st. helens in 1980.

8. Captain James Cook's ship ran aground on the great barrier reef in 1770.

9. We are moving to kentucky next year.

10. Kingsville, Texas, is in kleberg county.

EXERCISE B

11. My cousin is joining the united states air force when she graduates.

12. Our state elected members of the house of representatives.

13. The reporter wrote, "The Carrolton cougars cruised to an easy victory," but the game was tough!

14. Dr. Frye is a member of the american medical association.

15. This facility complies with the directives of osha and other regulatory agencies.

16. The interstate commerce commission regulated railroads.

17. Be sure to get on one of the buses that has "molltown isd" printed on its side.

18. The muscular dystrophy association educates the public about muscular dystrophy.

19. Did you apply to the university of pennsylvania?

20. Aren't we playing the hornets tomorrow?

Capitalization D, pp. 119–20

EXERCISE A

1. The algebra test is on monday.

2. I am watching the british open, my favorite golf tournament, this Sunday.

3. Why did the ming dynasty last for more than 250 years?

4. Marilyn, Maya, and I are cleaning up the park on arbor day this year.

5. Traditionally, seniors hold their formal banquet in early april.

6. This saturday is the day of the Expo.

7. This summer, Paul's birthday falls on a thursday.

8. We studied the battle of waterloo in history class today.

9. Why do the British celebrate guy fawkes day?

10. Our little brother Owen turns seven in january.

EXERCISE B

11. The greek chef cooked a delicious meal.

12. I am taking a course in asian studies next year.

13. The painting in the waiting area is by a little-known **j**apanese artist.

14. The curator's lecture concerned the history of the **i**roquois peoples.

15. Mara and David are studying **i**ndian culture in sociology class.

16. The commemoration of the birth of Jesus is called **c**hristmas.

17. We read selections from the **t**orah, the five books of Moses, in world religions class.

18. Muslims study the **k**oran, a book said to contain Allah's revelations to Mohammed.

19. One god in the Hindu religion is **v**ishnu.

20. A goddess of the ancient Greeks, **a**thena was thought to be wise.

Capitalization E, pp. 121–22

1. The new **c**omputers in the library were made by **d**ell.

2. She drives a **f**ord **p**ickup **t**ruck.

3. We took a **f**light on **n**orthwest **a**irlines when we visited Grandma.

4. Would you like some **o**atmeal—**q**uaker **o**ats—for breakfast?

5. The brand of **j**uice in the ice chest is **o**cean **s**pray.

6. She named her hot-air balloon **r**oswell.

7. We rode on a train called the **l**owland **f**lyer.

8. The **h**ubble **s**pace **t**elescope's optics were repaired in 1993.

9. One of Christopher Columbus's ships was named the **p**inta.

10. According to the story, the time machine **c**ounterclock visited ancient Rome.

11. On their quest for the Golden Fleece, the argonauts sailed aboard the **a**rgo.

12. Has **g**alileo's mission been completed?

13. The USS **f**orrestal sailed out of this port.

14. Footage of the launch of the space shuttle **c**olumbia was shown in a documentary last night.

15. It's fun to sit on the balcony listening to the sound of the train **n**ewcastle **e**xpress as it roars past our apartments.

16. My aunt visited Chaucer's grave, which is inside **w**estminster **a**bbey, when she was in London.

17. The senior prom was held at the **d**riskill **h**otel.

18. Meet us at the **p**aramount **t**heater at 7:00 P.M.

19. The **r**iverside **a**nimal **p**ark opened today.

20. The **t**urner **w**ildflower **c**enter was full of flowers in bloom.

Capitalization F, pp. 123–24

1. Who won the **p**ritzker **p**rize this year?

2. On our trip to Washington, D.C., we saw the **w**ashington **m**onument.

3. The **c**ivil **r**ights **m**emorial was dedicated in Montgomery, Alabama.

4. In Japan, the **s**engen **s**hrine has been used in the worship of Mount Fuji.

5. Someday, Brook hopes to win an **a**very **f**isher **p**rize.

6. Is neptune the planet farthest from the sun?

7. Studies of biela's comet helped support the idea that some meteors are pieces of comets.

8. The star proxima centauri is part of a triple star system.

9. The moon is too bright tonight for us to see the pleiades.

10. Like the moon, the planet mercury exhibits phases.

EXERCISE C

11. Do you enjoy your geometry II class?

12. I finished my chemistry homework last night.

13. Mr. Durand is a good french teacher.

14. I wrote an essay for my language arts class.

15. Mrs. Garcia is teaching physical education II next year.

Capitalization G, pp. 125–26

EXERCISE A

1. The mayor spoke to the town council.

2. My mother wrote a letter to sen. Maria Ochoa.

3. That sprained ankle may need a doctor's care.

4. The army troop was under the command of sergeant Jefferson.

5. Shelley was elected president of the student council.

EXERCISE B

6. Remember that grandma needs a ride to the airport at 3:00 P.M.

7. Is your mother coming to the talent show tonight?

8. I didn't know that your uncle Mike was in the Peace Corps.

9. This afternoon, dad, I have a guitar lesson.

10. My aunt Kelly was a country-western singer.

EXERCISE C

11. The *times* was founded in 1851.

12. My doctor keeps a copy of the book *middlemarch* on her desk.

13. Miguel told us that he found the painting *subway angels: a study in blue* very beautiful.

14. For Christmas, Ms. Kostas is writing a play called *a yuletide visitor.*

15. Have you finished reading the short story "the last bus"?

Chapter 13: Punctuation, pp. 127–44

End Marks, pp. 127–28

EXERCISE A

1. Maya said that it was nice being at home again.

2. Are you finished with your essay for history class?

3. Do you think your father will give us a ride to the movies?

4. We gathered research at the library on Saturday for our essays.

5. The newspaper was delivered early this morning.

6. What do you think of my handmade quilt?

7. Is it time for the baby's bath?

8. I would like more asparagus, please.

9. Is Michael's specialty spaghetti with marinara sauce?

10. Allison asked Teresa if Teresa could tutor her after school.

EXERCISE B

Answers may vary slightly.

11. No! Don't bring that spider near me!

12. Don't climb any higher.

13. My, what a beautiful garden that is.

14. That television is far too loud!

15. Hey! Turn that music down!

Abbreviations A, pp. 129–30

EXERCISE A

1. Did you read that book by F. Scott Fitzgerald?

2. My father is known as E. E. J. Serafini.

3. One of the U.S. presidents on the list is Ulysses S. Grant.

4. When Roberta becomes an author, her pen name will be R. N. McIntyre.

5. Of all the authors we have studied, I like E. M. Forster the best.

EXERCISE B

6. a
7. b
8. b
9. a
10. b

EXERCISE C

11. a
12. a
13. a
14. b
15. b

Abbreviations B, pp. 131–32

EXERCISE A

1. b
2. a
3. b
4. b
5. a

EXERCISE B

6. b
7. b
8. b
9. a
10. a

Commas A, pp. 133–34

The final comma in each series can be deleted, depending on teacher's instructions.

EXERCISE A

_C_ 1. Were Robert and Marcia and Janet the finalists in the talent show?

_____ 2. My favorite kinds of books are mysteries, thrillers, and the classics.

_____ 3. We rode our bikes, swam in the creek, and fished for trout.

_C_ **4.** Aunt Sally sewed and washed and pressed the curtains.

_C_ **5.** I wrote my essay and completed my math problems and planned my science project.

_____ **6.** Did Anna write, produce, and direct her own play?

_____ **7.** The cows grazed in the field, mooed loudly, and stood blinking in the sunlight.

_____ **8.** My father planted the flowers, mulched the garden, and watered the plants.

_C_ **9.** Vincent chopped the vegetables and stirred the stew and baked the bread.

_____ **10.** The parrot squawked, rustled its feathers, and asked for a cracker.

_C_ **11.** I like those light yellow curtains. [*or* I like those light, yellow curtains.]

_____ **12.** Lucy is a gentle, intelligent dog.

_____ **13.** Today was a beautiful, windy, spring day. (*or* beautiful, windy spring)

_____ **14.** Dad prepared a light, tasty lunch.

_____ **15.** Mario is a hungry, tired boy.

Commas B, pp. 135–36

EXERCISE A

1. Are you studying, or are you sleeping?

2. Patrick painted the shutters, and Felicia painted the eaves.

3. He didn't feel well, yet he went to the concert.

4. My uncle built a boat, but he isn't sure it will float.

5. We could go to the library, or we could study at home.

6. Veronica wasn't prepared for class, but she promised herself that it wouldn't happen again.

7. The kitten played with the toy mouse all day, so he took a long afternoon nap.

8. The book *The Hobbit* was very good, so I am reading *The Lord of the Rings*.

9. We went to the baseball game, and my little brother caught a fly ball.

10. I enjoyed the art gallery, and Mom enjoyed the wildflower center.

EXERCISE B

_C_ **11.** The snake sunned itself on the patio and then slithered away.

_____ **12.** The movie was long and dull, but my aunt stayed until the end.

_C_ **13.** Has Janet combined the colors and brushed paint on the canvas?

_C_ **14.** The newspaper flew from the delivery person's hand and landed right on the porch.

_C_ **15.** The leaf fell from the tree and tumbled in the wind.

_____ **16.** Little Sara swam the length of the pool, so her father cheered for her.

_____ **17.** I rode my bike to the bus stop, but I took a cab to the museum.

_____ **18.** Julian mixed the ingredients, and his mother baked the casserole.

_C_ **19.** Did Victoria kick the soccer ball and run down the field?

_C_ **20.** I read the article and wrote a review of it.

Commas C, pp. 137–38

EXERCISE A

_______ **1.** This pack, which was left on the table, belongs to Nancy.

___C___ **2.** Is this one of the lakes where migrating geese gather?

_______ **3.** Chip, who always worked hard at his studies, won a scholarship to Harvard.

_______ **4.** My bicycle, which needs a new tire, is leaning against the fence.

_______ **5.** Lyle, whose family lives in New York, plans to visit the city soon.

___C___ **6.** Holly is the only tennis player from Bayside High School who made it to the finals.

___C___ **7.** Jennifer wrote the article that was printed in the school newspaper.

___C___ **8.** We shouldn't try to paint the car's hood while the wind is blowing.

_______ **9.** That team, which is in our division, was last year's regional champion.

___C___ **10.** The store manager is the person whom we first contacted.

EXERCISE B

___C___ **11.** How many of the parts worn by friction can be replaced quickly?

_______ **12.** The snail, creeping slowly, finally made it to the garden.

___C___ **13.** Citizens needing information about where to vote should visit the city's Web site.

_______ **14.** Polished with wax, the car looked as if it were new.

___C___ **15.** The boy speaking with the teacher about the essay is Robert.

Commas D, pp. 139–40

EXERCISE A

1. Well, Sheila said that it might happen.

2. Why, that is the prettiest bouquet of flowers I have ever seen!

3. Yes, I will meet you at the movies at 7 P.M.

4. Oh, that was a complete surprise!

5. Yes, I agree with you completely.

EXERCISE B

6. Proofreading his essay for the last time, Julio felt happy about his work.

7. Blushing, Maura thanked the student council for their compliments.

8. Made from scratch, the casserole tasted delicious.

9. Smiling, the mayor, wearing his best suit, announced that the resolution had passed.

10. Trimmed, the bushes along the front sidewalk looked good again.

EXERCISE C

11. After warming up on the violin for the next several minutes, Frederick will perform.

12. When you get home, will you please let the dog out?

13. Although we didn't think we would win the game, we won by five points.

14. Near the edge of the lake, the ducks quacked happily.

15. Once the dog had drunk its water, did it bound off after the ball?

16. After we wash the dishes, we can ride our bikes to the park.

17. By the time the game is over, my mother should be here.

18. Since I have been exercising regularly, I feel healthier and stronger.

19. As soon as we feed the baby, we can leave for the picnic.

20. Beneath the books on the table, you will find the letter.

Commas E, pp. 141–42

EXERCISE A

_______ **1.** Your aunt, the one that lives in Mexico, is a talented artist.

___C___ **2.** Does the store Kodie's sell hand-crafted shelves?

_______ **3.** Barney, my little brother's hamster, runs on its wheel for hours.

_______ **4.** These tools, some wrenches and screwdrivers, are probably all we'll need to finish the project.

_______ **5.** The assignment, a five-page essay on wildlife, is due on Monday.

_______ **6.** My teacher, Ms. Janowitz, offered extra help on this algebra problem. [_or_ C]

_______ **7.** The quilt, the one with the gingham and clouds, was sewn by my great-grandmother.

_______ **8.** Is that dress, the white chiffon, the one you want?

_______ **9.** My dog, Barkley, is the smartest dog on the whole block. [_or_ C]

_______ **10.** The dentist, Dr. Nobles, always kids me out of being afraid. [_or_ C]

EXERCISE B

11. This pasta primavera, Dad, is the best I have ever tasted.

12. Your poem, Mr. Reyes, is inspirational.

13. Suzi, what do you think of our science project?

14. I will decorate for the party, Lee, if you bring the plates and cups.

15. What time does the movie start, Francis?

EXERCISE C

16. David went home, I believe.

17. In the first place, I never said that I could attend.

18. The tires, however, still need to be rotated.

19. She was, incidentally, the best cook in Springfield.

20. I agree with you, of course.

Commas F, pp. 143–44

EXERCISE A

1. The observatory will be built on Fifth Street / in Weston.

2. The address on the envelope read 234 Anderson Avenue, New York, NY / 65342.

3. Stop by my house at 875 / Beechwood Avenue.

4. The wellness center is at 543 Bluebonnet Lane, Marshall, TX 74652.

5. On January 30, 2018, my baby nephew will be eighteen years old.

EXERCISE B

6. Sincerely,

7. Dear James,

8. Very truly yours,

9. Regards,

10. Dear Aunt Janet,

EXERCISE C

11. Maria Cypress, M.D.

12. Patrick Matthews, Jr.

13. Antonio Martinelli, Jr.

14. Frederick Jefferson, Sr.

15. Anna Bledsoe, Ph.D.

Chapter 14: Punctuation, pp. 145–66

Semicolons A, pp. 145–46

EXERCISE A

1. I reached into my pocket; the horse nuzzled me for a treat.

2. The ice cubes must be ready; they have been in the freezer for an hour.

3. Patrick glanced at his watch; the plane was actually early.

4. The thermometer showed it was 100 degrees outside; Carla went back for her hat.

5. The player kicked toward the net; the goalie sprang toward the ball.

6. Dusk fell on the neighborhood; porch lights flicked on.

7. The school bus came to a stop; children poured out.

8. Margo felt relieved; her exam was over at last.

9. The probe landed on the planet; computers soon lit up with incoming information.

10. Sunshine Café is famous; people come from miles around for the food.

EXERCISE B

11. Laurie worked all summer; consequently, she started a savings account.

12. The nest we were observing was unusual; for instance, a hair ribbon was wound through it.

13. One team took the mountain route; meanwhile, our team took the river route.

14. The woven rug had a snag; it began to unravel, in fact.

15. The class was almost over; the students, therefore, put away the lab materials.

16. The weather forecast predicted rain; Miss Rose, accordingly, decided to bring her umbrella.

17. Don't throw that paper away; instead, put it in the recycling bin.

18. Linda was never a stranger for very long; in other words, she was very friendly.

19. It's getting dark out; besides, it's freezing outside!

20. That bird feeder is popular; sparrows, for example, flock around it every day.

Semicolons B, pp. 147–48

EXERCISE A

1. The suitcase contained shirts, lots of socks, pants, and a tie; but it had no identification card, tag, or paper inside.

2. Mr. Snyder will go on vacation June 16 through June 20, and then take off June 25; or he will take off June 6 through June 15.

3. A stage costume may have feathers, sequins, and several flounces; yet bright colors and a simple design will show up more onstage.

4. Stock your pantry with noodles, cans of fruit, dried beans, and rice; for you can use these inexpensive and healthy foods in so many quick meals.

5. The cave tour wound through low walkways, tight tunnels, and cramped turns; but then, at the end, we reached an open, large cavern.

6. The children gathered strawberries, blueberries, and raspberries; but the strawberries, sweet and juicy, were their favorites.

7. Mrs. Bird had stocked the cabinet with paper, envelopes, and pens; so the faculty, staff, and students did not run out of supplies.

8. Today's mail had two flyers, a few bills, and a catalog; yet no letters, postcards, or packages arrived.

9. On the lunch special you can order a main dish, two side dishes, and a drink; or a main dish, three side dishes, and fruit can be ordered.

10. The tournament runs Thursday, Friday, and Saturday; but Monday, and possibly Tuesday, will also be game days.

11. The museum displayed a mummy, from Egypt, a kimono, from Japan, and a statue, from Italy.

12. The band was made up of Shari Bolt, on piano, Chris Lee, on saxophone, Jon Burk, on guitar, and Cam Smith, on drums.

13. A baseball catcher wears a mask, to protect his face, a mitt, to protect his hand, and leg pads, to protect his knees.

14. My grandfather has lived in London, England, Berlin, Germany, and Dublin, Ireland.

15. The hit songs now are "Hello You," by Kate Katz, "Summer Song," by The Urchins, and "Salza Waltz," by Lemon-Aide.

Colons, pp. 149–50

1. The dentist had the following three openings: Tuesday morning, Thursday morning, or Friday afternoon.

2. The Colorado River crosses through Colorado, Utah, and Arizona.

3. The client jotted down the name, the address, and the phone number of the company.

4. The past club presidents were as follows: Mr. Samson, Miss Gonzales, and Mrs. Lee.

5. The trainer recommended several exercises as follows: sit-ups, curls, and pull-ups.

6. My father lives by these simple words: "You should not live your life as an explanation but live it as an exclamation."

7. That puppy was on a mission: Trashing the couch, chewing shoes, and shredding newspapers seemed its goal in life.

8. The store has a rigid policy: They accept no returns without a receipt and a price tag.

9. The novel *Lord Jim* begins with a description of Jim: "He was an inch, perhaps two, under six feet, powerfully built, and he advanced straight at you with a slight stoop of the shoulders, head forward, and a fixed from-under stare which made you think of a charging bull."

10. There's just one problem with this map: It is missing a section.

11. I believe that verse is from Mark 4: 1–15 in the Bible.

12. Sasha calls this painting *Hours of the Day: Siesta.*

13. The shuttle leaves at exactly 4:00 P.M. each day.

14. Books-Mart has a copy of *Mind Benders: Puzzles for Kids.*

15. Dear Madam Justice:

Italics, pp. 151–52

1. We finally got tickets to the musical <u>The Producers.</u>

2. Which part of the long poem <u>The Rime of the Ancient Mariner</u> did you enjoy most?

3. During my drive from work, I listen to <u>Fresh Air with Terry Gross</u> on the radio.

4. Have you seen my copy of <u>Time</u> magazine?

5. I'm learning sign language from the CD-ROM <u>Speaking with Your Hands.</u>

6. Will we rent <u>Antz</u> or some other movie this weekend?

7. Louisa always carries a tattered copy of <u>Jane Eyre</u> when she travels.

8. I get a laugh out of <u>The Far Side</u> cartoons on my desk calendar.

9. Is my costume for <u>A Midsummer Night's Dream</u> ready yet?

10. The new television series <u>Danger Mountain</u> should be a hit.

EXERCISE B

11. A replica of the <u>Mayflower</u> is on display in the harbor.

12. Carmen wrote <u>60</u> on the box, but I find only fifty candles in here.

13. We saw gorgeous scenery as we chugged along on the <u>California Zephyr</u>.

14. In Hawaii, we were greeted with the word <u>aloha</u> wherever we went.

15. Did I put an extra <u>s</u> in *Mississippi*?

Quotation Marks A, pp.153–54

EXERCISE A

1. "The secret to light biscuits is sticky dough," the cook confessed.

2. "I ride every day," the cyclist said, "and I eat a lot of high-energy meals."

3. "Let's try that scene again," said the director.

4. "Try a scarf with that jacket," the salesperson suggested.

5. The salesperson suggested, "That red scarf would match best."

6. "Race cars," said the mechanic, "need a lot of maintenance."

7. "Do not stand up in a canoe," our river guide warned.

8. The innkeeper apologized, "I'm afraid we are full tonight."

9. "Get your cold drinks right here," called the vendor.

10. "I think it's odd," Gene remarked, "how the newspaper always ends up in the doghouse."

EXERCISE B

11. "Is it going to rain?" Ivan wondered.

12. "The sky this morning," Eva wrote, "is pearly gray."

13. "This book," Kayla remarked, "says that pandas aren't actually bears."

14. "Don't forget to lock the door!" called Dad.

15. "May I have another serving, please?" the guest asked.

Quotation Marks B, pp. 155–56

EXERCISE A

1. Ann Smith appeared in the episode "Edge of Night" of *Mummies and Mommies*.

2. One of Elvis Presley's first hits was the song "Heartbreak Hotel" in 1956.

3. Every senior should read the article "Packing for College" in *On the Move* magazine.

4. Set the VCR to record the episode "Eleanor Roosevelt" of *The Lives of First Ladies*.

5. I made copies of the essay "My Certain Slant of Light."

6. Check the chapter "Fast Fish Recipes" in that cookbook.

7. Mrs. Forest read aloud Wallace Stevens' poem "Anecdote of the Jar" to the class.

8. The speaker in Lucille Clifton's poem "Island Mary" is a woman.

9. Do you understand that chapter called "Fire and Ice" in this novel?

10. "Wishing Star" is my favorite song on this CD.

EXERCISE B

11. Does your brother really prefer "snail-mail" to electronic communication?

12. The pilot radioed "roger" when he'd gotten our message.

13. In Canada, a "toonie" is a two-dollar coin.

14. The headings in the beautiful, old manuscript were set in a "swash" style of type.

15. Dan said he was a spelunker, which means "cave explorer."

16. The newspaper called the unsuccessful track meet an "Uh-Oh-lympics."

17. Gina loves to put little "emoticons" (smiling face symbols) in her e-mails.

18. *Voyage to Mars* was the "sleeper" hit of the summer movie season.

19. Dad's lawn mower is so advanced that we call it the "Robomower."

20. I think our cat is the original "couch potato."

EXERCISE A

1. The skater cautioned, "The ice is thin over there ~~near the trees.~~"

2. Rachel told the store manager, "I've read all the books in this mystery series. ~~I especially liked the first two mysteries.~~ Now I'm waiting for the next book to come out."

3. As Amy opened the mailbox, she thought, "Please, let there be a letter ~~from Greenwood College~~ telling me I'm accepted at the college."

4. The coach yelled, "Take your time. ~~That's it.~~ Nice shot!"

5. The skier asked, "~~Is it true s~~now can turn pink when it has red bacteria in it?" [S]

6. The naturalist wrote in his journal, "At midnight the coyotes began to howl. Their chorus of yips and yowls ~~kept me awake for hours. It~~ was music to my ears."

7. "That cloud ~~up there~~ looks full of rain," Sam noticed warily.

8. The artist murmured, "~~I think a touch of r~~ed makes a sunset more realistic." [R]

9. "Watch ~~my black Labrador~~ Cinder catch this ball," Ron called.

10. Darcy shivered, "Turn up the heat. ~~It's too cold in here.~~ I'm turning into an ice cube!"

EXERCISE B

Answers may vary.

11. "I think your drawing is ... very creative," Maria carefully commented.

12. Mrs. Parks sighed wearily, "Well ... at least *that's* over for another year."

13. After Tim drove for an hour, Keri asked, "Um ... do you know where you're going?"

14. Lance told Mrs. Ramirez, "That's right ... the dog ate my homework."

15. "No ... but you're getting warmer," Emma teased as Josie tried to guess her surprise.

Apostrophes A, pp. 159–60

EXERCISE A

1. volcano's
2. pioneers'
3. windows'
4. Odysseus'
5. Jerry's
6. trees'
7. player's
8. hive's
9. peacock's
10. women's

EXERCISE B

11. their
12. anybody's
13. Nobody's
14. his
15. their
16. no one's
17. our
18. everybody's
19. Your
20. Somebody's

Apostrophes B, pp. 161–62

EXERCISE A

1. That's
2. '96
3. What'll
4. We'd
5. o'clock
6. shouldn't
7. couldn't
8. Let's
9. I'm
10. Hasn't

EXERCISE B

11. *$*'s

12. *s*'s

13. *m*'s

14. *yes*'s

15. *please*'s

16. COD's

17. *9*'s

18. A's

19. X's

20. @'s

Hyphens, pp. 163–64

EXERCISE A

1. *none*

2. rum |mag |ing

3. *none*

4. pre |pare

5. foot |ball

EXERCISE B

6. *C*

7. two-way

8. world-famous

9. mayor-elect

10. all-points

11. salt-free

12. pre-Civil War

13. trans-Alaskan

14. *C*

15. five-eighths

Dashes, Parentheses, and Brackets, pp. 165–66

EXERCISE A

1. Only one word can describe the dance—fantastic!

2. Those salmon—look at them go—are swimming upstream.

3. Chen didn't just win any old award—he won the *top* award.

4. Then, a limousine drove up and—but I won't give away the show's end.

5. Ben Franklin—or was it William Shakespeare?—said the world is a stage.

EXERCISE B

6. Glenda Jones (formerly an actress) directed the movie *Modern Poetry*.

7. The menu offers two choices (I like either one) of vegetables.

8. Black bears (see their range map on page 50) still live in North America.

9. Polynesia (which means "many islands") lies in the Pacific Ocean.

10. Friday's assembly (I won't be able to attend it) will be in the gym.

EXERCISE C

Some answers may vary.

11. According to this article, "Few people expressed any opinion about President Tafft." [*sic*]

12. Chariot races (run on an oval track) were a popular event in ancient Rome. [*called a "hippodrome"*]

13. The skateboard (first developed in California) was originally used for surfing practice. [*in the 1930's*]

14. The story of Frankenstein (created by Mary Shelley) is a popular movie theme. [*who published it in 1818*]

15. "Franklin Roosevelt (who made public radio broadcasts) was president for twelve years," explained the tour guide. [*called 'fireside chats'*]

Words with *ie* and *ei,* pp. 167–68

EXERCISE A
 1. receive
 2. believed
 3. Weigh
 4. siege
 5. freight
 6. achievement
 7. eight
 8. sleigh
 9. shield
10. piece

EXERCISE B
11. niece
12. field
13. retrieve
14. heights
15. weird
16. foreign
17. brief
18. receipt
19. heifer
20. reign

Prefixes and Suffixes, pp. 169–70

EXERCISE A
 1. carefully
 2. rewrite
 3. semicircle
 4. loneliness
 5. overachieve

EXERCISE B
 6. conspiring
 7. excitement
 8. driver
 9. retrieval
10. sameness

EXERCISE C
11. allied
12. tried
13. reliable
14. delaying
15. emptiness

EXERCISE D
16. selected
17. trimmed
18. controllable
19. brightest
20. dropped

Plurals of Nouns A, pp. 171–72

EXERCISE A
 1. rings
 2. trenches
 3. foxes
 4. impressions
 5. guesses
 6. physicians
 7. fires
 8. canyons
 9. dishes
10. moons

EXERCISE B
11. enemies
12. keys
13. pantries
14. Mondays
15. decoys
16. candies
17. valleys
18. harmonies
19. attorneys
20. victories

EXERCISE C
21. lives
22. giraffes
23. beliefs
24. hoofs *or* hooves
25. shelves

Plurals of Nouns B, pp. 173–74

EXERCISE A

1. rodeos
2. torpedoes
3. trios
4. cameos
5. echoes

EXERCISE B

6. feet
7. spacecraft
8. men
9. pants
10. series

EXERCISE C

11. runners-up
12. baby sitters
13. bookshelves
14. window boxes
15. great-grandmothers

EXERCISE D

16. *although*s *or* *although*'s
17. formulas *or* formulae
18. 1870s *or* 1870's
19. @s *or* @'s
20. *W*s *or* *W*'s

Writing Numbers, pp. 175–76

EXERCISE A

1. There are <u>29</u> rows in this section.
2. C
3. <u>2</u> or <u>3</u> hours from now, we'll be leaving for the beach.
4. The flower garden has over <u>25</u> different types of flowers.
5. <u>475</u> actors tried out for the play.

EXERCISE B

6. The two runners tied for <u>3rd</u> place.
7. C
8. Jupiter, the <u>5th</u> planet from the sun, is larger than the <u>6th</u> planet from the sun, Saturn.
9. <u>1st</u>, put away your books and take out a pencil.
10. The game was boring until the bottom of the <u>8th</u> inning.

EXERCISE C

11. The ruins date to about <u>five hundred</u> B.C.
12. U.S. Highway <u>Five</u> runs from the Canadian border to the Mexican border.
13. Were you born in <u>nineteen ninety</u>?
14. C
15. Who can paraphrase lines <u>nine–twelve</u> of the poem?

Words Often Confused A, pp. 177–78

EXERCISE A

1. altogether
2. all together
3. already
4. all together
5. all ready

EXERCISE B

6. break
7. coarse
8. capital
9. course
10. brake
11. capital
12. break
13. capital
14. course
15. capital

Words Often Confused B, pp. 179–80

EXERCISE A

1. complements
2. desert
3. compliments
4. dessert
5. desert

Exercise B
6. its
7. loose
8. lead
9. It's
10. lead
11. lose
12. its
13. leads
14. lose
15. its

Words Often Confused C, pp. 181–82

Exercise A
1. quite
2. quiet
3. past
4. past
5. quite

Exercise B
6. than
7. whose
8. their
9. Who's
10. than
11. whose
12. There
13. then
14. They're
15. than

Chapter 16: Correcting Common Errors

Common Errors Review, pp. 183–84

EXERCISE A

Some answers may vary.

1. As graduation approaches, me [I] and many of my classmates have started to look for jobs.

2. I would like to work at Rapid Repair during the summer and gain most [more] experience fixing cars than I have at this time.

3. I am taking a course at my high school, which covers advanced topics in automotive repair, currently.

4. I can do basic tune-ups real good [really well], and I have alot [a great deal] of experience replacing brake pads and shoes.

5. Everyone which [who] works on late model cars needs to know their [his or her] way around computer diagnostics, and I would like to learn more about using computer diagnostics.

6. My experience and my desire to learn more automotive repair makes [make] me the perfect candidate for the job opening at Rapid Repair garage.

7. Because I have did [done] so well in my automotive repair classes, my teacher, Mr. Calhoun, has written me a letter of recommendation for this job.

8. I have included his letter, and you had ought to [should] call him if you have any questions about them [it].

9. I will graduate at the end of this month, and than [then] I will be available for work.

10. I can't [can] hardly wait to hear from you and begin my career as a mechanic. Thank you for taking the time to look over my application.

EXERCISE B

Some answers may vary.

11. After driving for six hours, we arrived at the campsite and managed to set up camp before nightfall, now everything is quite [quiet].

12. Its [It's] so beautiful hear [here]. The early morning fog makes me feel as though Im [I'm] waking in an enchanted land.

13. Ms. hughes [Hughes], our Trail Guide [trail guide], said that she hopes all of us will leave with a greater appreciation of nature and its beauty.

14. I have learned several new skills, how to set up a tent, how to read a compass, and how to identify different animals [animals'] tracks.

15. What a great time Im [I'm] having on this trip!

Chapter 17: Writing Clear Sentences, pp. 185–90

Using Parallel Structure, pp. 185–86

EXERCISE A

1. N	6. N
2. N	7. P
3. P	8. N
4. N	9. N
5. N	10. P

EXERCISE B

Answers may vary. Sample answers are provided.

11. Greeting visitors, answering questions, and directing people to different exhibits were three of my job duties at the children's museum.

12. The termites not only damaged several sections of the fence but also damaged the garage.

13. In the play review, the critic claimed that neither the special effects nor the elaborate costumes could hide the flaws in actors' performances.

14. Does Francine enjoy her ballet lessons as much as her tap class?

15. Either repainting the walls or replacing the dark curtains would help lighten up the room.

Complete Sentences and Sentence Fragments, pp. 187–88

EXERCISE A

1. S	6. S
2. F	7. F
3. F	8. F
4. S	9. F
5. F	10. S

EXERCISE B

Answers will vary. Sample answers are provided.

11. Taking the entire company by surprise, the president resigned.

12. When you are finished with the book, please put it with the others, which are stacked neatly on the desk.

13. Although the detective was puzzled by the odd message, she hoped eventually to understand its meaning.

14. That oak tree, the tallest tree on the block, must be at least one hundred years old.

15. My backpack was found lying on the steps of the museum.

Run-on Sentences, pp. 189–90

EXERCISE A

1. R
2. R
3. C
4. R
5. R

EXERCISE B

6. 3
7. 2
8. 1
9. 2
10. 4

EXERCISE C

Answers will vary. Sample answers are provided.

11. I have never seen a shark at the beach; however, I have caught sharks while deep-sea fishing.

12. American cranberries grow wild in the northeastern United States, but they are also grown commercially for beverage and food products.

13. Put on plenty of sunscreen before working in the yard. You don't want to get a sunburn!

14. Some spiders hunt their prey; others use webs to capture their prey.

15. That was the most exciting basketball game ever. That last-minute basket was amazing!

Chapter 18: Combining Sentences, pp. 191–96

Combining Sentences by Inserting Words and Phrases, pp. 191–92

EXERCISE A

Answers may vary slightly.

1. The planes landed carefully because of the rainy weather.
2. Granddad graciously helped Tomás with his project.
3. The greasy, worn hammer slipped from Marge's hand.
4. It felt nice to walk in the warm, soft sand.
5. Did the news anchor comment seriously on the story?

EXERCISE B

Answers may vary slightly.

6. "Ouch!" the boy yelled at the top of his lungs.
7. Football, a popular sport in this nation, is serious business at many high schools.
8. Scribbling furiously, the engineer jotted down a new idea.
9. Terrell met his goal to graduate early.
10. Has the pasta been boiling for about eight minutes?

Combining Sentences by Coordinating Ideas, pp. 193–94

EXERCISE A

Answers may vary.

1. Math and handwriting are far from their thoughts.
2. However, they go to the library often and read every day.
3. Who is thirsty and would like a drink of ice water?
4. Leon and Kim wore plenty of sunscreen.
5. When summer ends, the children and the teachers will go back to school.

EXERCISE B

Answers will vary.

6. Do boa constrictors live in Brazil, or do they live in Venezuela?
7. First, the marine biologists checked on the dolphins, but they needed to look in on the sharks, too.
8. This basketball needs more air; however, that one bounces well.
9. The carousel horses are over a hundred years old; therefore, they must be restored carefully.
10. Hattie took the bran muffins out of the tin; she topped each with fresh berries.

Combining Sentences by Subordinating Ideas, pp. 195–96

EXERCISE A

1. First prize went to those brothers who built a model of the Eiffel Tower out of matchsticks and sugar cubes.
2. The center ring featured an acrobat who wore a sparkling, sequined costume.
3. Have you heard the news that the concert's date has been changed?
4. Martha bought a nice gift for her friend who is moving to another state.
5. These jeans, which I ordered online, fit perfectly.

EXERCISE B

Answers may vary.

6. The water in the pool didn't warm up until the sun finally came out.
7. Because it had become so hot outside, Anna put her hair up in a ponytail.
8. The huskies dug holes in the snow so that they could sleep warmly.
9. After the racers passed the finish line one by one, the reporters tried to interview them.
10. As soon as the snow began to melt, the daffodils popped through the soil.

Chapter 19: Improving Sentence Style, pp. 197–202

Varying Sentence Beginnings, pp. 197–98

EXERCISE A

Answers will vary. Sample answers are given.

1. Yesterday,
2. Effortlessly,
3. Craftily,
4. Later,
5. Thirstily,

EXERCISE B

Answers will vary. Sample answers are given.

6. In the alpine meadows,
7. To achieve a goal,
8. Despite the rainy weather,
9. Gripping the lid,
10. Along with the students,

EXERCISE C

Answers will vary. Sample answers are given.

11. Because New York City is such a big place,
12. Although you could spend weeks in New York City,
13. In order to make the most of your time,
14. As soon as you arrive,
15. Provided that you follow this advice,

Varying Sentence Structure, pp. 199–200

EXERCISE A

1. CD
2. CX
3. S
4. CX
5. CD-CX

EXERCISE B

Answers may vary. Sample answers are given.

6. Tom goes to tutoring after school because he wants to pass all his courses.
7. Tom likes math best of all subjects, especially geometry.
8. Although history is not Maya's favorite subject, she gets good grades in it; however, she would rather study biology.

9. Sharon is a good friend, and she helped me study these words for my Spanish I exam.
10. Jenna likes reading literature in her English class and thinks American literature is best.

Revising to Reduce Wordiness, pp. 201–202

EXERCISE A

Answers may vary. Sample answers are given.

1. Because
2. nominated
3. afraid
4. Gratefully,
5. recommend

EXERCISE B

Answers may vary. Sample answers are given.

6. conifers
7. flour, yeast, milk, and salt
8. in his P.E. class
9. comic books and magazines
10. splashing about wildly on the end of the line

EXERCISE C

Answers will vary. Sample answers are given.

11. Alisha sneezed <u>and sneezed</u> repeatedly while walking through the meadow.
12. Do you ever suffer from hay fever or <u>suffer from</u> other allergies?
13. Nora loves to have fresh flowers, <u>blossoms only recently cut,</u> in her home.
14. Some people sneeze and sniffle when they are around cats, <u>which make them sneeze a lot.</u>
15. I'm glad to say <u>that I'm happy</u> I'm not allergic to our little terriers!

Resources, pp. 203–204

Manuscript Form, pp. 203–204

Students should have transferred information given in the exercise to the appropriate lines on the model page.